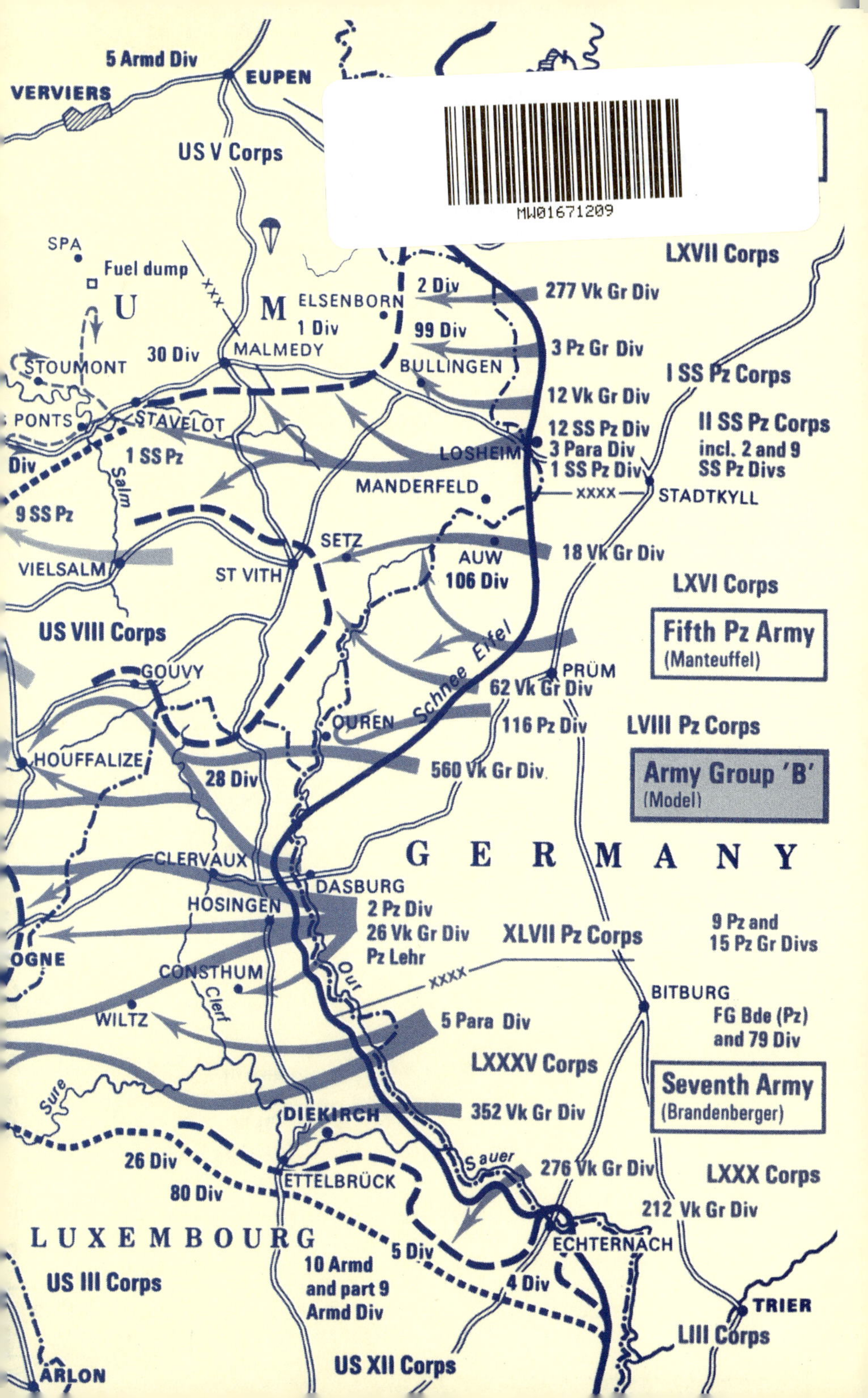
5 Armd Div
VERVIERS
EUPEN
US V Corps
SPA
Fuel dump
U
M
ELSENBORN
2 Div
277 Vk Gr Div
LXVII Corps
1 Div
99 Div
3 Pz Gr Div
30 Div
MALMEDY
STOUMONT
BULLINGEN
I SS Pz Corps
12 Vk Gr Div
PONTS
STAVELOT
12 SS Pz Div
3 Para Div
1 SS Pz Div
II SS Pz Corps
incl. 2 and 9
SS Pz Divs
LOSHEIM
Div
1 SS Pz
Salm
MANDERFELD
STADTKYLL
9 SS Pz
SETZ
AUW
18 Vk Gr Div
VIELSALM
ST VITH
106 Div
LXVI Corps
US VIII Corps
Fifth Pz Army
(Manteuffel)
Schnee Eifel
GOUVY
PRÜM
62 Vk Gr Div
OUREN
116 Pz Div
LVIII Pz Corps
HOUFFALIZE
560 Vk Gr Div
Army Group 'B'
(Model)
28 Div
G E R M A N Y
CLERVAUX
DASBURG
HOSINGEN
2 Pz Div
26 Vk Gr Div
Pz Lehr
XLVII Pz Corps
9 Pz and
15 Pz Gr Divs
OGNE
CONSTHUM
Our
Clerf
BITBURG
WILTZ
5 Para Div
FG Bde (Pz)
and 79 Div
LXXXV Corps
Seventh Army
(Brandenberger)
Sure
DIEKIRCH
352 Vk Gr Div
26 Div
ETTELBRÜCK
Sauer
276 Vk Gr Div
LXXX Corps
80 Div
212 Vk Gr Div
L U X E M B O U R G
ECHTERNACH
5 Div
10 Armd
and part 9
Armd Div
4 Div
US III Corps
TRIER
LIII Corps
US XII Corps
ARLON

"**M**r. Axelrod has written an excellent book about Patton's leadership skills, his approach to winning, his personal attitude, and his methods for results. These are lessons that can be learned and applied in the business community with great ease.

If your library does not contain *Patton On Leadership: Strategic Lessons for Corporate Warfare,* by Alan Axelrod, then your library is not complete.

Buy this book, study it, and follow its teachings. You will be a better manager for it."

CHARLES M. PROVINCE
President/Founder The George S. Patton, Jr. Historical Society

"**P**atton is the personification of leadership projected through the force of personality.

Patton on Leadership provides valuable insights into the precepts of this celebrated twentieth century warrior."

AL KALTMAN
Author of Cigars, Whiskey & Winning
Leadership Lessons from General Ulysses S. Grant

"**W**hat can a civilian corporate leader learn from the combat tactics of General George S. Patton, Jr.? Find out by reading Alan Axelrod's *Patton on Leadership*. He takes the leadership wisdom of one of America's greatest and most colorful combat Generals and applies it to contemporary civilian corporate organizations. Organized around Patton's quotations and writings, each being related to specific corporate situations, Axelrod presents an in-depth understanding into the General's leadership style and demonstrates that Patton's 'genius was being able to capitalize on his own intuitive notion of leadership.' This book provides a perceptive insight of a leadership methodology that may be a valuable asset to many corporate executives."

RUTHERFORD B. JOHNSON
Commander, Georgia Chapter
George S. Patton, Jr. Historical Society

"**A**s Sergeant (and Manager) of the Second Armored Division Officers' Club in Ft. Benning, Georgia, I frequently had personal contact with General Patton.

Alan Axelrod is right on target with his description of the General and the comparison to corporate warfare. I recommend reading it."

1ST LT. HENRY L. SOBEL
U.S. Army (Ret.) 01010072

PATTON ON LEADERSHIP

STRATEGIC LESSONS
FOR CORPORATE WARFARE

PATTON ON LEADERSHIP

STRATEGIC LESSONS FOR CORPORATE WARFARE

ALAN AXELROD

PRENTICE HALL PRESS

Library of Congress Cataloging-in-Publication Data

Axelrod, Alan.
Patton on leadership : strategic lessons for corporate warfare / Alan Axelrod.
p. cm.
ISBN 0-7352-0091-2 (cloth)
1. Leadership. 2. Industrial management. 3. Strategic planning. 4. Patton, George S. (George Smith), 1885-1945. I. Title.
HD57.7.A96 1999
658.4'092—dc21 99-28533
CIP

PHOTO CREDITS

Credit to Charles M. Province, President and Founder of the General George S. Patton, Jr. Historical Society for the following:
Map on title page, chapter openers and endpapers
Title page insert photo
Insert photo of Patton on chapter 1 opener
Medal and insignia on opening panel

All other photos are courtesy of the Patton Museum of Cavalry and Armor, Fort Knox, Kentucky.

Acquisitions Editor: *Tom Power*
Production Editor: *Eve Mossman*
Formatting: *Robyn Beckerman*
Interior Design: *Suzanne Behnke*

Printed in the United States of America

10 9 8 7 6 5 4

ISBN 0-7352-0091-2

PRENTICE HALL PRESS
Paramus, NJ 07652

On the World Wide Web at http://www.phdirect.com

US First Army
(Hodges)
US VII Corps
US VIII Corps
US XVIII Abn Corps
DINANT
CINEY
DURBUY
WERBOMONT
TROIS PONTS
GRANDMENIL
HOTTON
VIELSALM
ROCHEFORT
LAROCHE
HOUFFALIZE
STADTKYLL
LXVI Corps
11

Contents

Foreword

No less a management thinker than Peter Drucker wrote almost a half-century ago, that the first systematic book on leadership, written more than 2000 years ago by Xenophon, was still the best. Xenophon was a Greek general, and his writings concerned combat leadership.

What is the special attraction of battle leadership that a business writer of the stature of Drucker would recommend it for study by all managers? Most Hollywood movies would have it that battle leadership is simply running around and shouting orders which others instantly obey. Real combat leaders know better.

Battle is a worst case condition in which the risks are high, the uncertainty great, and the hardships and "workplace conditions" are unknown in any other field of human endeavor. If these weren't enough, battle is probably the only leadership environment in which both followers and leaders would rather be somewhere else. In these extremely challenging situations, successful combat leaders help those they lead to accomplish almost incredible feats and cause them to perform at almost superhuman levels of productivity. Moreover, they do this while assuming responsibility for their followers' lives and welfare, and risking their own lives as well. No wonder Drucker was impressed. For this reason, some years ago, I accepted the challenge to try to explain how to adapt this form of leadership to achievement in other areas, and I wrote *The Art of the Leader* (Prentice Hall, 1990) and *The Stuff of Heroes* (Longstreet Press, 1998).

In many ways, Alan Axelrod's challenge in writing Patton on Leadership was even greater. For as Axelrod correctly notes in his introduction, George S. Patton was not only one of this country's greatest military leaders, but by dint of accomplishment, must be considered one of history's outstanding commanders. For here was a leader who not only got things done, but got things done faster, more decisively, and most importantly, at a lower cost in that most important and cruelest price of warfare, the lives of his soldiers, than anyone else.

Yet, Patton did not finish the war with all the rewards given others. When Patton died in a tragic accident after the fighting had stopped in Europe, he was a senior commander, but did not wear the five stars achieved by a number of his World War II contemporaries. Also, his last command was not the combat command he desired in the Pacific, but an administrative one in Europe that was mostly paper and in which his talents laid untapped. He had more than once been severely reprimanded by his friend and fellow West Pointer, Dwight David Eisenhower who was his highest commander in Europe. And even today, with his exploits denied by none, he remains controversial. For with all his abilities, Patton was not perfect. And his leadership skills, which were of the highest order, were sometimes marred by equally great faults. These sometimes led him to actions that would have terminated the career of a lesser general.

And therein lies the difficulty of anyone who seeks to duplicate or even learn from Patton's feats and to apply them not only on the battlefield, but in the boardroom, and in other organizations. Patton's genius and his flaws are so closely intertwined that they are almost impossible to separate.

But successful leaders do what unsuccessful leaders simply won't do. And in so doing, they frequently achieve the impossible. In this mold, Alan Axelrod has achieved what others may have thought to be impossible, and he has done so in a magnificent fashion. Like Patton, Axelrod has prepared well before battle. His research has been both deep and thorough. Whereas other historians have researched Patton to prepare a biography, Axelrod has researched Patton to extract what all leaders can learn from his remarkable achievements. He has dissected him through Patton's own writings, his actions, and what others have written about him. He has developed a total portrait of what Patton accomplished and discovered how he accomplished it. Then he has moved on to the monumental task of cataloging Patton's leadership beliefs and showing us examples of these beliefs in action. Finally, and most importantly, Axelrod has shown us how to apply Patton's talents in leading our own organizations.

In rapid fire Axelrod gives us twenty-four of Patton's dimensions of leadership, from the qualities of great leadership and generalship to the most important tasks of every leader. He explains fifteen approaches to developing a winning attitude, forty-one insights into analysis, preparation, and planning, sixteen discussions on execution, forty-nine recommendations on training, mentoring, motivating, and inspiring, and sixteen suggestions on communication and coordination. Having discovered perhaps more of Patton's beliefs on leadership than any other researcher, Axelrod goes on to tell us exactly how Patton went about creating efficiency, what he believed about courage and character, and perhaps most importantly, how Patton went about "managing the impossible."

I learned a lot from this book, and you will too. I recommend *Patton on Leadership* to anyone who would assume the mantle and take up the trust of leadership.

William A. Cohen, Ph.D.
Major General, USAFR, Ret.

Introduction

Mention George S. Patton to a group of executives or managers and you are likely to get two kinds of responses: unqualified disparagement or unqualified praise. The disparagers bring up the infamous "slapping incident," in which Patton, visiting wounded men in a field hospital, verbally assaulted and then slapped the helmet off a soldier who had no physical injuries but was suffering from battle fatigue. Patton declared that he would not have "cowards" in his army. (There were actually two similar incidents, but the public remembers them as one.) Beyond this, most disparagers have nothing more *specific* to say against Patton, save that he was "arrogant" or "pompous" or "not well liked by his men" or that he swore—well, that he swore like a soldier.

Those who admire Patton are quick to admit such flaws, but then they point out that these are part of what made him an extraordinary leader. If he slapped a soldier, well, it was certainly wrong, but he thought it necessary for the morale of the other troops. He was tough. War is tough. Leaders have to be tough. He drove his army hard, yes, and he made many enemies among colleagues and subordinates, but he also produced results. He was indeed arrogant, but sometimes a good leader *has* to be larger than life. And so on.

But the fact is that, again typically, Patton's admirers are no more specific in their praise than are his disparagers in their criticism. Anyway, both parties more than likely have formed their picture of Patton from seeing the extraordinary, seven-Oscar-winning film starring George C. Scott as the general. This isn't a bad thing. *Patton* is a great movie, and as a result of it, no American general, not Grant, not Eisenhower, not even Schwarzkopf or Colin Powell, is better known. Patton died in 1945; the war he fought ended more than a half-century ago, but nevertheless, mention of his name still evokes strong reaction pro and con.

That reaction is emotional, strong but vague and ill-defined. It does not get at what makes Patton worth remembering.

What *does* make Patton worth remembering?

The *results* he produced.

- ★ He was the major architect, builder, organizer, and master tactician of mechanized warfare (the use of "armor"—that is, tanks).
- ★ In the largest, most ambitious military training maneuvers the U.S. Army had ever staged, on the eve of the nation's entry into World War II, Patton outgeneraled all of his colleagues and, furthermore, demonstrated that he had forged a more effective fighting force than anyone else had.
- ★ Patton transformed an utterly defeated and thoroughly demoralized American force in North Africa into an army capable of defeating the Nazis' most brilliant general, Erwin Rommel, the feared "Desert Fox."
- ★ Patton invaded Sicily with lightning speed that outstripped even the British general Sir Bernard Law Montgomery, and, considering the magnitude of his accomplishment, he did so with minimal casualties.
- ★ As commander of the Third Army, Patton drove across France and into Germany at a breakneck pace, destroying more of the enemy and liberating more towns than any other unit in World War II or, for that matter, in the history of American arms.
- ★ During this drive, when a surprise German offensive threatened to wipe out the 101st Airborne and other units (the Battle of the Bulge), Patton performed a tactical miracle, turning his troops, exhausted from three months of forced march and continual battle, 90 degrees north to launch a bold counterattack into the southern flank of the German army. The Battle of the Bulge was thereby transformed into a U.S. victory.

How did Patton produce such results?

This man, so often accused of vainglory and arrogance, was always the first to explain that "his" success had been achieved not by him, but by his army. He had trained, motivated, and led his troops to outstanding feats of performance and productivity. Patton was, in short, a superb manager.

All that Patton's detractors criticize him for is true. His many flaws make him human and approachable. Indeed, he had more problems than even his harshest critics identify. For example, Patton suffered from dyslexia, yet managed to survive the academic rigors of West Point. Like all too many men and women of his time, Patton was a bigot and racist, yet he racially integrated his Third Army when the rest of the U.S. armed forces (except, to a limited degree, for the navy) were strictly segregated. He was a hidebound conservative overly worshipful of tradition, yet he was the most innovative of commanders and the army's leading champion of cutting-edge mechanized warfare.

Patton's human failings, and, more important, how he overcame and even *used* those failings, make him much more approachable as an exemplar of management and management style than, say, Washington or Lincoln, who seem to occupy a realm beyond that of mere mortals.

Any manager—anyone who directs a company or department or supervises others in any way—would benefit from reading as much as possible about George S. Patton. The trouble is that Patton himself wrote little (though what he wrote is choice) and that others wrote much about him. If you're a working manager, it's a sure bet you don't have a lot of time for reading, let alone ferreting out the good stuff on Patton. That's where this book will help. It presents Patton's key pronouncements on leadership, along with what others, who knew and worked with Patton, recognized as his leadership style and technique.

For convenience, the book is divided into ten parts. The first part provides background on Patton the man and Patton the military leader. The other nine parts approach the subject of leadership thematically, presenting the best of Patton on

- ★ The dimensions of leadership
- ★ Developing a winning attitude
- ★ Getting the facts and making plans
- ★ Execution and opportunity
- ★ Mentoring, motivating, and inspiring
- ★ Communication and coordination
- ★ Creating efficiency
- ★ Courage and character
- ★ Managing the impossible

Most of the brief "chapters" in these nine parts consist of a quotation by or about Patton, followed by a discussion of just what the quotation can teach us about management and leadership. Together, these make up a set of brief lessons on management and leadership, which all managers can use and apply immediately

- ★ To develop a leadership attitude
- ★ To develop leadership skills
- ★ To develop a leadership image
- ★ To develop and exhibit personal dynamism
- ★ To communicate effectively in words
- ★ To communicate effectively with body language
- ★ To establish priorities
- ★ To set objectives and goals
- ★ To inspire others
- ★ To manipulate others ethically
- ★ To create loyalty
- ★ To build a team
- ★ To resolve conflict effectively

- ✯ To be an effective coach and mentor
- ✯ To lead by example while minimizing micromanagement
- ✯ To nurture creative thought in others
- ✯ To know the "enemy" (your competition)
- ✯ To create outstanding production
- ✯ To create maximum performance
- ✯ To create exceptional quality

Patton on Leadership does not have to be read cover to cover. Dip in where you will, although I do suggest that you start with the first part: "What He Did and Who He Was" for an overview that sets the rest of the book in a more meaningful context.

Preface

One might easily question the selection of New York Yankees owner George Steinbrenner to compose the preface to the book, *Patton on Leadership*. After all, I was only 15 years old when General Patton died.

Perhaps it is because the late renowned Howard Cosell frequently referred to me as "Patton in Pinstripes" on national television, or perhaps because I attended Culver Military Academy as a young man, finishing with a very undistinguished academic record except for Military Science, where I was an A+ student. Or perhaps because as a young Air Force Lieutenant in the '50s, a decade after his passing, I held George S. Patton as one of the finest of all American military leaders; and because today, as a student of military leadership, both good and bad, from Frederick the Great through the likes of Custer, Grant, Lee, Pershing, Eisenhower, and even Sitting Bull and Crazy Horse, to name a few, I consider General George S. Patton, with all his controversy, idiosyncrasies, and unpredictability, to be perhaps the greatest of them all—"the ultimate warrior."

When I first read about Patton, I was struck by the fact that he moved his troops farther and faster than anybody believed possible with so few casualties. As I read more about his leadership strategies—how he achieved these remarkable results—I became even more impressed. The confidence he instilled in his soldiers was legendary. The men under his command considered themselves to be "Patton's Men." They looked sharper, they fought tougher, and they were time and time again called upon to perform beyond perceivable limits. It was often said that his troops would accomplish the impossible, then go out and do it all over again. "Patton's Men" may not have always truly appreciated the man's leadership style at the time. Human nature is such that the discipline and the obedience required by a great leader are so often cause for griping and displeasure. But in retrospect, to have served under Patton was a red badge of courage to be worn forever.

When you talk baseball and a man in his later years describes himself by saying, "I am a former Major League ballplayer," that is one thing. But if he was a Yankee, he will almost always say, "I was a New York Yankee," not just a Major League ballplayer. A prominent sports editor from Pittsburgh once wrote: "There are never ex-Yankees. Their pinstripes assure them an immortal presence." The same should be said of Patton's men. They have an immortal presence because they served with one of the greatest generals this nation has ever known. I often talk to friends of mine who served in the Second World War. Time and again, I will hear them say that they served in the Fifth Army or the First Army, or in the Philippines or the European Theater. But if they were one of "Patton's Men," they make it very clear, "I served with Patton." That says it all as far as they are concerned.

Patton's leadership lessons ring as true today as they did when he was leading the Third Army across France and into Germany itself. His enduring message is one of preparation, teamwork, pride, motivation, and discipline—never asking his men to do anything that he himself would not do. These principles form a strong foundation for leading a successful army or any other form of endeavor. The outcome may not be life and death as it is in war, but General Patton's strategies are still sound and will help managers and leaders in all types of organizations achieve winning results.

Patton could reduce complex tasks to their essence, then focus all of his resources on that essence. He believed in attention to every detail. Put all the pieces in place, give your people every opportunity to succeed, and they will do so. Give people goals they can understand, they will meet them. Set the bar high and your people will raise themselves to meet it.

Patton drove his men fast and hard, but he also knew their limits. He would never push them beyond their capabilities, because that would be a foolish waste of resources and would result ultimately in defeat. In baseball, if a pitcher can consistently give you six strong innings, but begins to falter after that, you're asking for trouble if you try to force him to pitch a complete game.

Although some of Patton's detractors called him "reckless," he actually was a very careful and studious planner. He was a student of his opposition and their leadership. Before making a decision, he would gather all the facts he could and seek input from trusted advisors. He would study the appointed task from many angles, trying to spot the pitfalls as well as the advantages of various strategies. I can recall very clearly in the great movie *Patton* (which I probably have seen twenty times) when Patton is in the process of defeating Rommel's vaunted forces in North Africa on the field of battle. George C. Scott, playing Patton, bellows out as victory seems assured, "Ah Rommel, you magnificent bastard, I read your book." This indeed depicts Patton. He studied and prepared, and by understanding his opposition, once the decision was made, he wouldn't second-guess himself or express any doubt to others.

"Americans play to win at all times," Patton once said. "I wouldn't give a hoot in Hell for a man who lost and laughed." While baseball is certainly not the same as war, I still want my team to play to win at all times, to expect to win starting as Minor Leaguers, to develop a winning attitude in the tradition of the great Yankee teams of the past and present. And don't ever let me catch anybody on my team laughing in the locker room after a tough loss. I can see very close parallels between General Patton's philosophy and that of the great football coach Vince Lombardi who said: "Winning is not a sometime thing; it's an all-the-time thing. You don't win once in a while; you don't do things right once in a while; you do them right all the time. Winning is a habit. Unfortunately, so is losing."

I know from firsthand experience that many of Lombardi's top players, at times during the campaigns, detested his leadership and his genius. Packers' Hall-of-Fame defensive tackle Henry Jordan once said, "He treated us all the same. Like dogs." But now that the championships have been won by those great Packer teams, don't dare challenge or question Coach Lombardi to any of his ex-players. If you do, I can assure you, you'll regret it.

Patton's lessons on leadership are valuable guidelines that can be applied by managers in all walks of life, from the baseball diamond to the manufacturing plant to the corporate boardroom. There is no doubt in my mind that Patton, though he had numerous detractors, was what we refer to in sports as the "go-to man." When the ballgame or battle is on the line and when the odds against you seem almost insurmountable, the man you look to is your "go-to guy." Certainly it can be said that General George S. Patton was the Allies' "go-to-guy" in the Second World War and probably one of the greatest in the history of Military Science. I think you'll be as inspired as I have been in reading this book and studying the true genius of General George S. Patton.

George M. Steinbrenner III
Principal Owner of the New York Yankees

1

What He Did and Who He Was

Patton's Achievement and Background

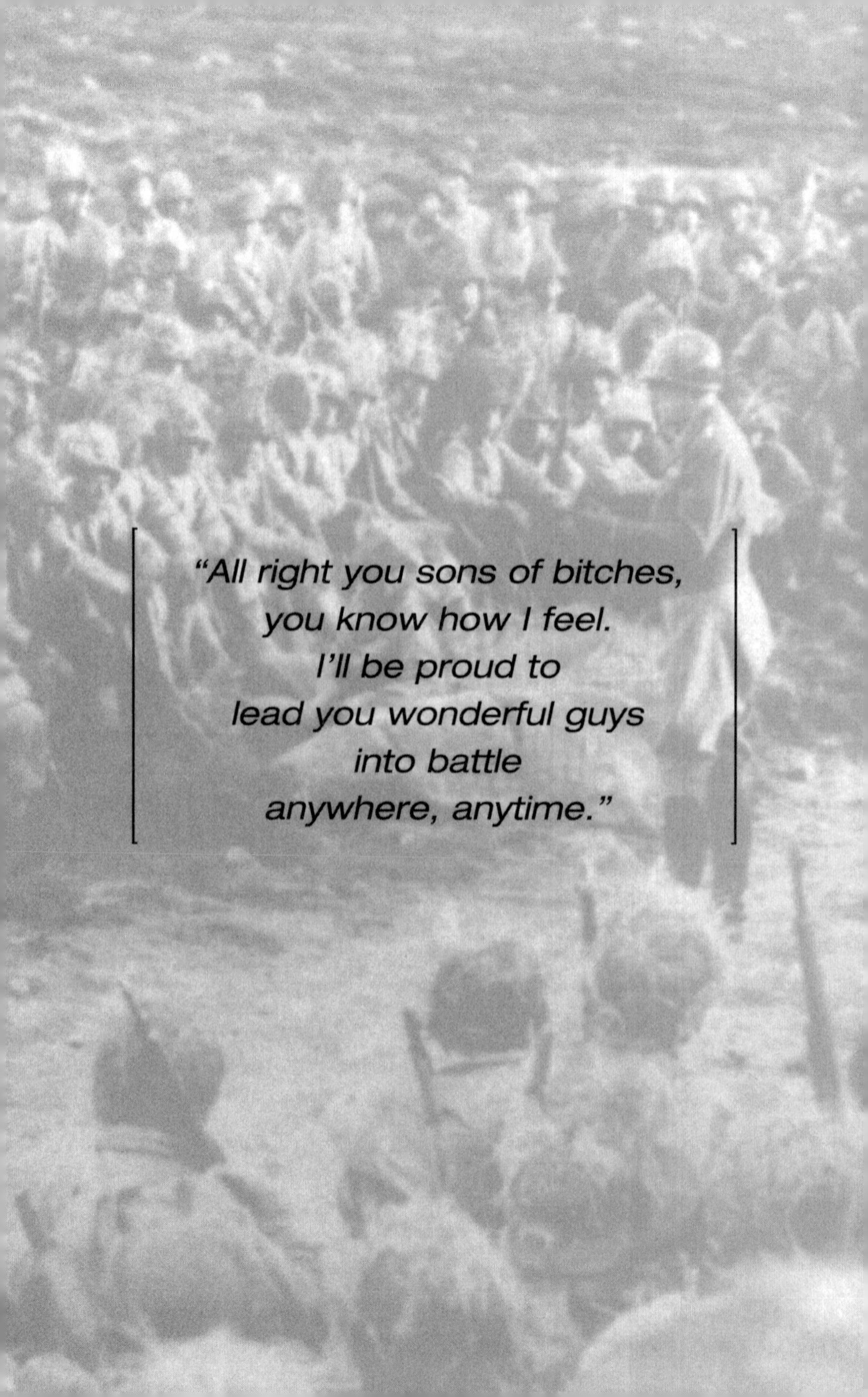

"All right you sons of bitches,
you know how I feel.
I'll be proud to
lead you wonderful guys
into battle
anywhere, anytime."

Patton as Management Guru

You've picked up this book, so I have to assume you're interested in the life and career of George Smith Patton, Jr., and, more particularly, what that life and career can tell you about your own. If you *are* interested in Patton, it's a pretty good bet that you've also seen George C. Scott play the general in *Patton*. The film's been around since 1970, so maybe you've seen it more than a few times. If so, you certainly recall the opening scene.

A giant American flag fills the screen. We hear the sound of footsteps, and Patton rises, step by step, to a stage in front of the flag. The camera surveys the details of his magnificent uniform, an array of impeccably placed ribbons and medals. Then onto the face of George C. Scott—almost a dead ringer for Patton—and an actor whose skill has captured what the general repeatedly described as his "war face," the unsmiling granite mien of a warrior, which Patton admitted practicing daily before a mirror.

Written by Francis Ford Coppola and Edmund H. North and directed by Franklin Schaffner, *Patton* is one of the great screen biographies, not only because of its artistry as film and its spiritual faithfulness to its subject, but for its historical accuracy as well. Read the writings of Patton, of those who knew the general, and of his biographers, and it is immediately apparent that much of the film's dialogue was drawn directly from Patton's own words. In that stirring opening scene, Scott delivers a speech that Patton made many times, with many variations—but never from written notes—during the days spanning March to July 1944, in preparation for the D-Day landing at Normandy. The version reproduced here is quoted from George Forty's *The Armies of George Patton:*

> *I want you men to remember that no bastard ever won a war by dying for his country. He won it by making the other dumb bastard die for his country. All this stuff you've heard*

about America not wanting to fight, wanting to stay out of this war, is a lot of horseshit. Americans love to fight. All real Americans love the sting of battle. When you were kids you all admired the champion marble shooter, the fastest runner, the big-league ball players, and the toughest boxers. Americans love a winner and will not tolerate a loser. Americans play to win all the time. I wouldn't give a hoot in Hell for a man who lost and laughed. That's why Americans have never lost and never will lose a war. The very thought of losing is hateful to Americans. An army is a team. It lives, eats, sleeps and fights as a team. This individuality stuff is a bunch of bullshit. The bastards who write it for the Saturday Evening Post, *don't know any more about real battle than they do about fucking. We have the finest food and equipment, the best spirit, and the best men in the world. I pity those poor bastards we're going up against. We're not just going to shoot the bastards, we're going to rip out their living goddamned guts and use them to grease the treads of our tanks. We're going to murder those lousy Hun bastards by the bushel basket.*

Some of you men are wondering whether or not you'll chicken out under fire. Don't worry about it. I can assure you that you'll all do your duty. The Nazis are the enemy. Wade into them. Spill their blood. Shoot them in the belly. When you put your hand into a bunch of goo, that a moment before was your best friend's face, you'll know what to do. There's another thing I want you to remember. I don't want any messages saying we're holding our position. We're advancing constantly and we're not interested in holding onto anything except the enemy. We're going to hold onto him by his balls and kick the hell out of him all the time. We're going through him like crap through a goose.

There's one thing you men will be able to say when you get back home. Thirty years from now, when you're sitting by your fireside, with your grandson on your knee and he asks: "What did you do in the great World War Two?" you won't have to shift him to the other knee, cough, and say, "Well, I shoveled shit in Louisiana."

I'm not supposed to be commanding this Army. I'm not even supposed to be in England. Let the first bastards to find out be the goddamn Germans. I want them to look up and howl, "Ach! It's the goddamn Third Army and that son-of-a-bitch Patton again!"

All right, you sons of bitches, you know how I feel. I'll be proud to lead you wonderful guys into battle anywhere, anytime. That's all.

Apart from its historical interest, why read this speech now? Without doubt, it is one of the great motivational speeches of World War II, but what can a manager learn from it?

Let's get one issue out of the way quickly. The profanity in this speech is certainly inappropriate in just about any modern work setting. Even if Human Resources wouldn't come huffing and puffing down our necks, few of us would feel inclined to use the words Patton uses here. (In a rare departure from the historical records, even the *Patton* filmmakers substituted the word *fornicating* for the Anglo-Saxon monosyllable Patton actually used.)

But let's go ahead and start with the language. Let's look beyond the four-letter words. The language of this speech is bold. It is direct. It is frank. Given the audience and the task that lay before that audience, it is, in fact, highly effective language. If Patton's leadership style might be reduced to a single formula, it would be this: Blend a commanding presence with a common touch. The magnificently uniformed Patton, his austere "war face" set hard, knew how to put himself above and apart from those he led, yet it was never so far apart or so far above them that he was perceived as anything other than one of the people he led. He always spoke of "fighting beside" his men. And he meant it just the way he phrased it.

Now, look farther beyond the shock value of the profane language. Look at how the speech begins. It commands attention by saying precisely the opposite of what all soldiers in all armies have wearily expected to hear since the Roman poet Horace (65-8 B.C.) wrote *"Dulce et decorum est pro patria mori"*—it is sweet and dignified to die for your country.

Instead, Patton says: "No bastard ever won a war by dying for his country. He won it by making the other dumb bastard die for his country."

In this opening statement, Patton introduces humor that rings with truth. He lets his troops know that he does not want them to die. What would be the value of that? But he does want them to kill. And he tunes this message precisely to the frequency of the hard-bitten, wise-cracking cynical persona that has always been associated with the American soldier: We're all dumb bastards. Yet Patton also elevates this persona, using it to motivate the behavior that he wants and the mission he demands. With his first sentence, the goal of war ceases to be some hollow, oft-repeated abstraction like "glory" or "sacrifice," but becomes instead a practical, immediate, individual issue of survival and victory.

Read further in the speech. The next thing Patton does is to give his audience an identity. He tells them who they are.

They are Americans.

Then he defines what it means to be an American, putting that definition in terms that these young men can well understand. He talks about the champion marble shooter, the fastest runner, the big-league ball player, and so on. Patton knows his audience—boys in their late teens and early twenties. And he must have asked himself: What is the experience of such an audience? It is the stuff of boyhood.

From this, Patton transforms the bewildering idea of an immense army locked in world-engulfing combat into something even boys like these can understand: The idea of a team.

Now the general goes on to say the kinds of things that gave him his nickname (a nickname, by the way, he loathed): "Old Blood and Guts." He talks about ripping out the entrails of the enemy and using them to grease the treads of our tanks. He talks about nothing less than brutal mass murder.

Such are the realities of war, and above all else he wants his troops to face reality. But note that he immediately follows this with assurances that these mere boys—who were themselves, a short while ago, shooting marbles rather than human beings—are in fact capable of doing what is being demanded of them. There is nothing uncertain about the way Patton puts it:

> *I can assure you that you'll all do your duty. The Nazis are the enemy. Wade into them. Spill their blood. Shoot them in the belly. When you put your hand into a bunch of goo, that a moment before was your best friend's face, you'll know what to do.*

He does not say, "I have confidence in you" or "I believe you can do this." He frames the bloody, terrifying mission as something that *will* be done. It is stated as an inevitability.

Now, keep reading the speech.

For, after defining the impending mission as something that —without doubt—*will* be accomplished, Patton suddenly takes his men 30 years into the future. He paints for them a picture, first and foremost, of their survival to be grandfathers. And it is not just survival, but comfortable, secure survival, bathed in the glow of glorious achievement that Patton states with the humor of utter sincerity. He does not wrap his audience in the flag. He does not tell them their "sacrifice" is making the "world safe for democracy." Nor does he tell them what they *will* or what they *should* tell the grandchildren perched on their knee. Instead, he simply tells them what they *won't* have to say: *"Well, I shoveled shit in Louisiana."*

The rest he leaves up to the pleasant fantasy of the individual.

The mark of a great motivational speaker is the ability to present ideas as if they come not from him or her, but from those who listen to him or her. Thus Patton presents his vision, but does so in a way that allows each of his hearers to make that vision their own. In this, he gives each man a personal stake in the battle to come.

The speech ends with the trademark Patton sincerity. The general had an uncanny ability to express powerful emotion without getting all mushy about it. Read that brief concluding paragraph again:

> *All right, you sons of bitches, you know how I feel. I'll be proud to lead you wonderful guys into battle anywhere, anytime. That's all.*

Who else but Patton could combine so movingly and effectively the phrases "you sons of bitches" and "you wonderful guys"?

Here endeth the lesson.

Okay. So George S. Patton, Jr., could make one pretty mean speech. As a motivational speaker, he could have held his own against Dale Carnegie, Werner Erhard, and Tony Robbins rolled into one.

Fine. But you're a *manager,* not a rider on the motivational speaking circuit. What else can you learn from this man Patton?

Patton would tell you that the only meaningful way to evaluate a leader and his or her methods is by looking at results. Let's start there. What exactly did General Patton *do,* anyway?

Patton is best remembered as the commanding general of the U.S. Third Army, an organization that varied in strength from about a quarter million personnel to 437,860 as its final campaign ended on May 8, 1945. From August 1, 1944, to April 30, 1945, a payroll of $240,539,569 was disbursed. During this same period, 1,234,529 long tons of supplies were brought into the Third Army area by rail, truck, and air. Within Third Army boundaries, 2,186,792 tons of supplies were transported a total distance of 141,081,336 miles. A total of 3,655,322 vehicles, carrying supplies for the troops, were clocked through 109 traffic-regulating points.

In terms of ammunition, 533,825 tons were received during 281 days of combat. Combat vehicles numbered 7,581, but Third Army Ordnance repaired a total of 21,761 combat vehicles during this period. Almost 30,000 general-purpose vehicles were issued to the Third Army.

Third Army engineers built 2,498 bridges of all descriptions—about 8.5 miles of bridges, total. They repaired or reconstructed 2,240 miles of road and 2,092 miles of railroad. The organization's Signal Corps laid 3,747 miles of open wire and 36,338 miles of underground cable. Its telephone operators handled an average of 13,986 calls daily.

Third Army ambulances carried 269,187 patients. Third Army officers administered civil affairs in Belgium, Czechoslovakia, France, and Luxembourg, as well as providing military governments for parts of Germany and Austria, to control about 30 million people.

But it is the battle record of the Third Army that is most telling.

The official account, *The Third Army's After Action Report,* begins: "In nine months and eight days of campaigning, Third U.S. Army compiled a record of offensive operations that could only be measured in superlatives, for not only did the Army's achievements astonish the world but its deeds in terms of figures challenged the imagination."

Patton was given command of the newly formed Third Army in January 1944 and arrived in France on July 6 to lead it in the breakout from Normandy, site of the D-Day landings, across France and into Germany. During the "nine months and eight days" the report speaks of, Patton's Third Army liberated or gained 81,522 square miles in France, 1,010 in Luxembourg, 156 in Belgium, 29,940 square miles in Germany, 3,485 in Czechoslovakia, and 2,103 in Austria. An estimated 12,000 cites, towns, and villages were liberated or captured, 27 of which contained more than 50,000 people. Moreover, during the last-ditch German Ardennes offensive, the so-called Battle of the Bulge, when the 101st U.S. Airborne Division was cut off and the Allied advance threatened, Patton wheeled his entire weary army 90 degrees to the north and launched a devastatingly successful counterattack in record time.

The Third Army captured 1,280,688 prisoners of war from August 1, 1944, to May 13, 1945. The enemy lost 47,500 killed and 115,700 wounded—with prisoners, a total of 1,443,888 casualties—to the Third Army, which incurred 160,692 casualties, including 27,104 killed, 86,267 wounded, 18,957 injured, and 28,237 missing—of whom many were later reported captured.

In short and in sum, the Third Army under General Patton went farther and faster than any other army in the history of warfare.

General Patton himself missed no opportunity to assign credit for the success of his campaign where he believed it belonged: with the personnel of the Third Army. Nineteen Medals of Honor, 291 Distinguished Service Crosses, 44 Distinguished Service Medals, 4,990 Silver Stars, 1,159 Legions of Merit, 247 Soldier's Medals, and 29,090 Bronze Stars were awarded to members of the Third Army. But Patton was their leader, and I have ladled on the summary facts and figures of the army's career to illustrate that, above all else, leading an organization of such massive proportions in a project at once enormous, hazardous, and in every way formidable requires an exercise of masterful management. Patton the great general was Patton the consummate manager. Only such modern organizations as General Motors Corporation (with 745,000 employees), Wal-Mart Stores (675,000 employees), and PepsiCo, Inc. (480,000) manage more personnel than Patton did when the Third Army was at maximum strength. As Patton himself once observed, beside war, all other human endeavor pales into puny insignificance.

So why not learn from the best?

The great pity is that Patton wrote no formal book-length treatise on command, although he did manage to compose a memoir, *War as I Knew It,* before he was fatally injured in an apparently minor automobile accident on December 9, 1945. A low-speed collision between his staff car and an army truck threw Patton forward off the back seat, breaking his neck. He died on December 21.

But the day-to-day remarks of a figure as dashing, influential, powerful, and colorful as Patton did not go unnoticed—or unrecorded. He was also a prolific writer of letters, orders, and memoranda, many of which contain gems of leadership and management observation and advice.

This book collects and presents Patton's leadership "lessons," based on his own writings and remarks and based on what others have said about him and the way he did things.

But a word of caution. As the speech quoted earlier makes abundantly clear, Patton was a highly unconventional person. He pulled no punches. He also relished delivering a shock. He delighted in the contradictions of his own personality. When a reporter, well aware of Patton's reputation for salty language, asked the general if it was true that he read the Bible, Patton replied, "Every goddamn day."

Few of us are in a position to emulate the Patton personality in all of its controversy. Few of us would want to. Many who served with him idolized him. Most who took a more objective view were still full of praise. General Lucian Truscott called him "perhaps the most colorful, as he was certainly the most outstanding battle leader of World War II." The British military biographer H. Essame observed that, "In terms of blood and iron, he personified the national genius which had raised the United States from humble beginnings to world power: the eagerness to seize opportunities and to exploit them to the full, the ruthless overriding of opposition, the love of the unconventional, the ingenious and the unorthodox, the will to win whatever the cost and, above all, in the shortest possible time." The historian Eric Larrabee wrote that "A commander must be able to 'think like' the unit he commands: All its weapons and their capabilities, the terrain on which it is disposed, the state of its supply and of its training and morale—in short, what it can reasonably be asked to do . . . all must be an extension of his own mind. . . . Patton could think like an army."

Yet, for all the praise, you don't have to look very far to find detractors, too. The cultural critic Dwight Macdonald called him "brutal and hysterical, coarse and affected, violent and empty," and Andy Rooney, of CBS Television's *60 Minutes,* made no secret of having "detested Patton and everything about the way he was. It was because we had so few soldiers like him that we won the war. . . . Patton was the kind of officer that our wartime enlisted man was smarter than. It was the independent action of the average GI that made our Army so successful . . . not the result of the kind of blind, thoughtless devotion to the next higher authority that Patton demanded." Then there was a soldier quoted in Carlo D'Este's biography, *Patton: A Genius for War,* who called the general "a swaggering bigmouth, a Fascist-minded aristocrat . . . compared to the dreary run of us, General Patton was quite mad."

Be forewarned, then, as you read the chapters that follow. Patton offered counsel to the bold, not the timid. His example is one to be followed selectively. But whatever his personal shortcomings—and they were many—Patton was a leader who got the job done, and did so with the least cost in lives and materiel.

A Life Story

George Smith Patton, Jr., was born November 11, 1885, on his father's ranch and vineyard, which was situated in Los Angeles County, spread out over what is today the city of Pasadena and much of the UCLA campus. He was a frail boy, greatly adored by his parents. With single-minded determination, he built up his strength and became a fine horseman and all-round athlete. He delighted in his father's stories about his Virginia ancestors, distinguished military men all. A great uncle, Waller Tazewell Patton, fought gallantly for the Confederate cause during the Civil War, suffering a severe wound at Second Bull Run and a fatal wound, at age 29, in Pickett's Charge during the battle of Gettysburg. George Smith Patton, the boy's grandfather, also fought for the Confederacy, falling in the Third Battle of Winchester on September 19, 1864.

Young George was clearly an intelligent boy, but he had an inordinate amount of trouble learning to read and write. Concerned that he would be mocked by classmates, Patton's parents educated him at home. In Patton's day, there was no name for the learning disorder now called dyslexia, a complex of learning problems that includes reading, writing, and spelling reversals as well as difficulty concentrating, hyperactivity, mood swings, and feelings of inferiority.

Dyslexics feel dumb and discouraged. It was, however, Patton's good fortune to have loving parents who did all they could to encourage their son. For his part, the dyslexia became an early enemy to fight and against which to achieve victory. Patton struggled to learn to read and, in fact, became an avid reader of history, especially military history. While his writing, even into adulthood, was littered with misspellings, Patton learned to express himself precisely and vividly. His fragmentary World War II memoir, *War as I Knew It,* is among the most readable firsthand accounts of the war.

Struggling through home schooling and then a private preparatory school, Patton decided to enroll at the Virginia Military Institute for a year in preparation for what he hoped would be an appointment to West Point. The appointment came, and Patton studied at the U.S. Military Academy from 1904 to 1909. They were years of intense academic struggle. Failing math his first semester, he had to repeat part of his first year, but Patton persevered, becoming a star athlete and cadet adjutant. He graduated from the Point in 1909 with a second lieutenant's commission.

After graduation, Patton served on a number of military posts, quickly acquiring a reputation for great energy and ability. He competed on the U.S. pentathlon team in the 1912 Olympics at Stockholm, Sweden, displaying singular prowess in the grueling competition that included a 300-meter swim, pistol shooting, a 4,000-meter run, fencing, and a 5,000-meter steeplechase. Although his fifth-place showing overall did not earn him a medal, Patton was praised by the Swedish newspapers, who noted that "his energy is incredible" and said of his fencing that it was "calm . . . and calculated. He was skillful in exploiting his opponent's every weakness."

Indeed, Patton's swordsmanship was extraordinary. He was chosen by the army to attend the French cavalry school at Saumur and was then sent back to the States to enroll in the Mounted Service School at Fort Riley, Kansas, in 1913. From 1914 to 1916, he served as an instructor at Fort Riley and was appointed Master of the Sword, with responsibility for writing the army's new saber manual. He even worked with the Ordnance Department to design a new sword for the calvary. Officially called U.S. Saber, M-1913, it soon came to be known informally and universally as the "Patton sword."

Lt. Patton was eager to see action, and in 1916 he served with Gen. John J. "Black Jack" Pershing in a "punitive expedition" against the Mexican revolutionary bandit Pancho Villa. Villa had executed 16 U.S. citizens in Mexico and then attacked the town of Columbus, New Mexico. President Woodrow Wilson dispatched Pershing to pursue and punish Villa, but, although members of the expedition—including Patton—clashed with Villa's followers, the wily revolutionary evaded capture. Nevertheless, Pershing was impressed with Patton, who was promoted to captain in 1917. For his part, Patton idolized Pershing as a mentor, his ideal of everything a commander should be.

In May, just one month after the United States entered World War I on April 2, 1917, Patton was assigned to Pershing's staff and was sent to France with the first contingent of the American Expeditionary Forces. Despite his great admiration for Pershing, Patton wanted a combat assignment rather than a staff job, and he became the first U.S. officer to receive tank training. At this time, tanks were a novelty, unreliable but promising, and it is a testament to Patton's vision that he eagerly sought to master the new weapon. Trained as a cavalryman, expert in the ancient art of swordsmanship, Patton now rushed to embrace the future.

Patton took to the tanks immediately, and no sooner was he himself trained than he was asked to set up the AEF Tank School at Langres, France, in November 1917, to train others. Promoted to temporary lieutenant colonel and then colonel, he organized and led the First Tank Brigade in the key battle against the Saint-Mihiel Salient (September 12–17, 1918), in which he was wounded. Patton also commanded tanks at Meuse-Argonne, the last offensive of the war (September 26 to November 11).

Returning to the United States in 1919, he reverted to the rank of captain but was quickly promoted to major and given command of the 304th Tank Brigade at Fort Meade, Maryland (1919–21). Unfortunately, the peacetime army had little interest in developing tanks, and Patton decided to return to the cavalry after he was offered a prestigious posting at Fort Myer, Virginia, where he served from 1921 to 1922. After graduating from the Command and General Staff School with honors in 1923, Patton was appointed to the army's general staff, serving until 1927. Appointed chief of cavalry in 1928, he left that post to attend the Army War College in 1932. During the 1930s, Patton achieved promotion to lieutenant colonel (1934) and then colonel (1937) and, after a stint commanding cavalry, was tapped for command of the Second Armored

Brigade in 1940. Promoted to temporary brigadier general and then temporary major general, he was given command of the Second Armored Division in April 1941.

With war looming, the United States had begun to mobilize, and, in June, massive maneuvers (war games) were organized in Tennessee. From July through September, even more ambitious maneuvers were staged in Louisiana and Texas, followed by further exercises in the Carolinas during October and November. Patton excelled in these maneuvers, emerging victorious from the war games and attracting the attention of his superiors.

But Patton soon had reason for mixed emotions about his spectacular showing. Eager to get into the fighting after Pearl Harbor (December 7, 1941), he was not immediately sent overseas, but assigned to what higher command considered a more important task: the creation of the Desert Training Center near Indio, California. U.S. military planners knew that they would first fight the Germans, not in Europe, but in North Africa, from which an invasion of Sicily, and then the Italian mainland, would be launched. The planners also realized that the army had absolutely no experience fighting in the desert, especially with tanks. From March 26 to July 30, 1942, Patton undertook the task of training a first generation of American desert fighters.

As brilliant a combat commander as he would certainly prove himself, Patton excelled in the training of troops. Wanting to be in the fight, he nevertheless wholeheartedly threw himself into the work at the Desert Training Center. His soldiers not only emerged as the best disciplined troops in the entire army, but they created, perfected, and learned the techniques of desert combat.

During August, Patton participated in the planning of Operation TORCH, the U.S. landings in North Africa. He personally commanded the Western Task Force in these landings, which took place on November 8, 1942. In March of the following year, he was called on to replace Gen. Lloyd R. Fredendall after II Corps suffered a stunning defeat at Kasserine Pass.

The crisis brought on by the Kasserine debacle was grave. Defeat in the first contest between the U.S. Army and the German

Afrika Korps under General Erwin Rommel, the famed "Desert Fox," was a severe blow to American military confidence.

Arriving at II Corps headquarters, Patton immediately sized up the problem as one of management and leadership. The troops were sloppy and unsoldierly, a rabble rather than an army. Patton instituted a tough regime aimed at achieving perfect discipline. He began by enforcing regulations governing uniforms, including the wearing of neckties, leggings, and helmets. As General Omar N. Bradley observed, "Each time a soldier knotted his necktie, threaded his leggings, and buckled on his heavy steel helmet, he was forcibly reminded that Patton had come to command the II Corps, that the pre-Kasserine days had ended, and that a tough new era had begun."

It was a first step toward making the men of II Corps feel like soldiers so that they would act like soldiers. In a remarkably short time, Patton managed to transform II Corps into a winning organization.

Patton's difficult personality resulted in friction with British allies, and he was transferred from command of II Corps to command of I Armored Corps, which grew into the Seventh Army. From July 10 through August 17, Patton drove this organization through a difficult but triumphant invasion of Sicily. At the height of his triumph came the incident for which he is still most notorious.

On August 3, Patton was delighted to learn that General Eisenhower was planning on awarding him the Distinguished Service Cross, and that afternoon he went to the Fifteenth Evacuation Hospital to visit with wounded troops. Patton always found such visits painful—he said that he felt that he was responsible for getting the men hurt—but he also believed that it was a commander's duty to make such personal visits.

Amid the gravely wounded men was Pvt. Charles H. Kuhl, who exhibited no visible wounds. Patton asked him what his problem was.

"I guess I can't take it."

Enraged, Patton swore at Kuhl, called him a coward, and ordered him out of the hospital tent. Frozen in place, the battle-fatigued soldier did not move. Patton slapped his face with a glove, raised him to his feet by his shirt collar, and sent him out of the tent with a kick in the rear.

That incident passed with no further consequence, but, on August tenth, during a visit to a different evac hospital, Patton ran across another victim of battle fatigue.

"It's my nerves," Pvt. Paul G. Bennett told the general.

"What did you say?"

"It's my nerves. I can't stand the shelling any more."

"Your nerves, hell, you are just a goddammed coward. I ought to shoot you myself right now," Patton continued. Reaching for his trademark ivory-handled revolver, he pulled it out of its holster and waved it in front of the terrified soldier. Then he delivered a slap across Bennett's face.

It was this second incident that ignited a firestorm of public and professional criticism and outrage, which very nearly resulted in Patton's being relieved of command. As it was, Eisenhower ordered Patton to make the rounds of every Seventh Army unit and apologize for the incident. He apologized personally to Bennett and to Kuhl, neither of whom seemed to feel any resentment for what Patton had done. An eyewitness even remarked on how Kuhl's face "lit up with a broad grin. He grabbed and shook the general's hand. . . . It was very dramatic."

But the "slapping incident" kept Patton out of the action until January 1944, when he was sent to England and given command of the newly formed Third Army. While in England, he was used as a decoy to make the Germans think that he was to lead an invasion of France, not from the beaches of Normandy, but across the Pas de Calais. The ruse worked, and Hitler ordered most of the strength of the German forces concentrated at Calais rather than at Normandy, where the D-Day landings actually took place.

It was after the landings that Patton arrived on the continent to lead the breakout from Normandy across France. These were Patton's glory days and a great chapter in the history of the United States Army. We have addressed the campaign in the introduction: a drive through France and into Germany unprecedented in terms of ground liberated or captured, distance covered, and speed of execution. As if this weren't miracle enough, Patton turned his nearly half-million-man army on a dime to make a forced march north to Bastogne, where a surprise German offensive had pinned down the entire 101st Airborne Division and threatened to derail the Allied advance into Germany.

From January through March 1945, Patton advanced across the Rhine and pushed into central Germany and northern Bavaria. By V-E Day, the German surrender on May 8, 1945, Patton's Third Army had penetrated as far as Linz, Austria, and Pilsen, Czechoslovakia.

With the war in Europe won, Patton hoped to be sent to the Pacific to participate in the conclusion of the war against Japan. But the supreme commander in that theater, General Douglas MacArthur, would never stand for "competition" from a general like Patton. Instead, Patton was assigned as military governor of Bavaria, an assignment for which this combat commander was utterly unsuited. He elicited an outcry from the press and the public first by his denigrating, mistrustful, and critical attitude toward the Soviet allies (privately, he thought it advisable to turn the U.S. Army *against* "the Communists") and then by his practice of putting former Nazis in administrative positions in the provisional Bavarian government. This was strictly against the Allies' "de-Nazification" policy, but Patton pointed out that the ex-Nazis were the only people with the training and experience to run vital government services.

In October 1945, amid growing protest and friction, Patton was relieved as Third Army commander and given command of the Fifteenth Army, largely a "paper" organization, the chief duty of which was to compile a history of the war in Europe. Although greatly discouraged by this turn of events, Patton went about his new assignment diligently, until he suffered his fatal injury on a road near Mannheim on December 9.

It was only—and immediately—after his death in a Heidelberg military hospital on December 21 that his colleagues and the nation rallied around his memory, as if they had all suddenly realized what

Patton had accomplished: Nothing less than the spearhead thrust that had defeated Nazi Germany, that had liberated much of Europe, and that, for many, brought an end to the Holocaust.

George S. Patton, Jr., was buried in Hamm, Luxembourg, in the thick, red clay of the Ardennes, in a grave alongside those of many of his men who had perished in the Battle of the Bulge.

2

"A Commander Will Command"

On the Dimensions of Leadership

"When in doubt attack"

1. Definition of Leadership

A commander will command.

What does it mean to command—or to manage? Look at this deceptively simple phrase, which Patton often spoke. It looks like a tautology, one of those maddening definitions that define a word in terms of itself. What does a commander do? He commands.

But that leaves out the verb *will*. The commander *will* command. He has no choice. That is what he does. If he does not do it, he is not a commander.

The first rule of commanding is to *act* as if you are in charge—because you are. When Patton arrived in Indio, California, to take command of the Desert Training Center on January 15, 1942, he was ushered in by a motorcade with sirens screaming. Patton's staff staged a precise military ceremony, and, as Lt. Porter B. Williamson, recalls:

> *Coming into our area was a shiny World War II command car—no top, two seats and a bar on the front seat to give support when riding in a standing position in the back seat. Standing erect at the bar was Gen. Patton! The command car stopped in front of the men from the 2nd Armored Division. Gen. Patton ignored us; not even a glance or smile in our direction. As he dismounted from the command car, one of our officers whispered, "Here comes a tear jerking speech!"*

But there was no speech. Instead, Patton silently oversaw the ceremony of raising "bright new flags." Then, at eleven, the precise hour appointed for him to take command, he "suddenly saluted us. We returned his salute, and he started speaking: 'I assume command of the I Armored Corps! At ease!'"

Not a word from Gen. Patton, such as, "Glad to be aboard!" "Glad to join you!" or "We will make a great team!" Nothing was said as we waited for Gen. Patton to speak again.

Still at attention, Gen. Patton commenced, "We are in a long war against a tough enemy. We must train millions of men to be soldiers! We must make them tough in mind and body, and they must be trained to kill. As officers we will give leadership in becoming tough physically and mentally. Every man in this command will be able to run a mile in fifteen minutes with a full military pack including a rifle!"

One of our overweight senior officers chuckled.

"Damn it!" Gen. Patton shouted, "I mean every man of this command! Every officer and enlisted man—staff and command; every man will run a mile! We will start running from this point in exactly thirty minutes! I will lead!"

It pays to analyze this scene with some care. Patton has often been accused of egotism and self-dramatization. To the first term he would probably object, but not to the second. He insisted that a commander should look like a commander. He practiced what he called his "war face"—stern and unsmiling—in front of a mirror. He not only functioned as a commander, he *acted* like one. Asked to describe her greatest experience on stage, the famed British actress Lynn Fontanne did not talk about one of her appearances with husband Alfred Lunt in some great play, but about when she was appearing in Paris toward the end of World War II:

We had finished our show and we were taking our curtain calls when someone in the audience shouted, "Gen. Patton is here!" The house lights were dim, so I could not see the audience. I went to the microphone and asked, "Would Gen. Patton please come on stage, if you are here?"

> *. . . My first glimpse of him was as he came from the right side of the stage. He was tall, and with his uniform and medals he seemed too tall to come through the door. He was wearing his shiny helmet, which he removed as he came on stage. I was sure the roof would fly away as the audience cheers increased when he stepped in full view of the audience. I stepped back to offer the microphone to him. He winked and nodded his head to me. I shall never forget it! He marched half-way towards me, stopped, clicked his heels, and saluted the audience as he held his helmet over his heart with his left hand. The cheering increased. He held the salute for the perfect amount of time. When he lowered his hand salute, he turned sharply and walked off stage. He did not say a word—never smiled nor gave a polite wave of his hand! As an actor his timing was perfect. His salute was the perfect "speech" to give to such an audience. . . . Beyond doubt that cheering for Gen. Patton was my greatest experience on stage!*

Patton, then, was not afraid to *act* like a commander. He set himself apart from his "audience," as any great actor does. Yet he did not stop there. Return to the moment of his taking command at Indio. He was at once aloof—a remote, austere, resplendent figure of command. But then he immediately gave an order. No hesitation. No discussion. A command. A commander *will* command.

Most important, his first order demanded performance from his subordinates, *and* his first order included himself. The order demanded that all officers—himself included—be able to perform to the level that was being demanded of the enlisted men, the personnel the officers were expected to command. In a sense, then, this order suddenly reduced everyone to the same level, including Patton himself.

But only for a moment. "I will lead," Patton's order concluded. Even as he leveled himself, his officers, and his men, he asserted absolute leadership. Patton was fond of declaring that "Every soldier is a four-star army," that an army is its *soldiers,* not its commanders. Yet he always asserted his leadership position.

The effective leader performs the miracle of a great actor: He sets himself apart from those he commands even as he identifies with those he commands.

Now, Patton has often been accused of being a micromanager, of getting involved in every detail of running his army. This is partly true, but partly an illusion. In fact, Patton believed in training a person to do his or her job and then getting out of the way. Patton wrote that senior commanders had a "habit of commanding too far down."

> *Actually, a General should command one echelon [level] down, and know the position of units two echelons down. For example, an Army Commander should command corps, and show on his battle map the locations of corps and divisions, but he should not command the division. A Corps Commander should command divisions and show on his map the location of combat teams. A Division Commander should command combat teams and show on his map the location of battalions. . . . It has been my observation that any general officer who violates this rule and at, let us say, the Army level, shows the location of battalions, starts commanding them and loses his efficiency.*

Yet, in his insistence on seeing the big picture, on not losing sight of the forest for the trees or losing command of the army for the battalions, Patton also insisted that senior officers, himself included, "get up front." They were not to remain glued to a map in headquarters.

> *I want every member of this staff to get up front at least once every day. You will never know what is going on unless you can hear the whistle of the bullets. You must lead the men. It is easier to lead than to push. Besides, having you senior colonels up front is a great incentive and temptation for the younger officers. Nothing like creating a vacancy to get a promotion!*

Patton continued:

> *Trying to lead men from behind makes you a driver and not a leader. It is easier to lead men just as it is easier to pull a log chain. You cannot push a log chain and you cannot push troops. The troops will keep running back to you for instructions—really from fear. A leader has to be ahead of his men. You've got to know what is going on all the time. You cannot swim without being in the water! You cannot ice skate without being on the ice. No one ever learned to skate on a map board. Take the map with you and get up front!*

On one occasion, Patton returned to headquarters from the front lines. He called a senior colonel over to a map, marked a point on a river, and declared, "Cross the river at this point."

"General, we have little information about the depth of the river at that spot. We would probably have to build a pontoon bridge, and we do not know the soil conditions of the banks."

"We will cross where I made the mark! Every man can walk across, and I am certain the tanks can get enough solid ground to drive across. The banks are solid. The river is wide but quite shallow."

"How can you be sure, General?"

"Take a look at my pants! That's how shallow the water is. I walked across without collecting any enemy fire!"

This is vintage Patton, *commanding.*

2. Qualities of a Great General

1. *Tactically aggressive (loves a fight)*
2. *Strength of character*
3. *Steadiness of purpose*
4. *Acceptance of responsibility*
5. *Energy*
6. *Good health*

—INSCRIBED BY WEST POINT CADET PATTON
IN HIS COPY OF THE TEXTBOOK *ELEMENTS OF STRATEGY*

If you think of these six items as the requisites of leadership—and not just of military leadership—they make for a provocative list. Items two through six should provoke no controversy, but putting the love of a fight as number one will not find universal favor. These days, most managers like to talk about compromise and accommodation. To be sure, such actions are appropriate in some situations. But the fact is that leadership also requires a willingness to be aggressive. In a small minority of situations, an aggressive attitude is necessary in dealing with people. Most of the time, however, "tactical aggressiveness" is an attitude toward working a problem. It describes a leadership approach that actively engages reality rather than passively waiting for favorable circumstances to shape themselves. In business, the aggressive leader *creates* favorable circumstances.

3. A Model Leader

Under the personal supervision of the General every unit . . . every horse and every man was fit; weaklings had gone; baggage was still at the minimum, and discipline was perfect. When I speak of supervision, I do not mean the nebulous staff control so frequently connected with the work. . . . General Pershing knew to the minutest detail each of the subjects in which he demanded practice and by his physical presence and personal example and explanation insured himself that they were correctly carried out.

—PATTON ON GEN. JOHN J. PERSHING

In this description of the commanding officer under whom he had served during the "Punitive Expedition" against Pancho Villa, and in France, during World War I, Patton sums up the chief qualities of leadership:

1. Perfection of detail
2. Personal supervision
3. Thorough and detailed knowledge of the business at hand
4. A strong physical leadership presence
5. The ability to set a personal example
6. The ability to communicate—explain—orders
7. The commitment to ensure that orders are correctly executed

4. The Greatest General

The greatest general is he who makes the fewest mistakes—i.e., he who neither neglects an opportunity nor offers one.

—NAPOLEON, PARAPHRASED BY PATTON IN HIS READING NOTES

Just what interested Patton about Napoleon's pronouncement? It is not just the definition of the greatest general, but also the definition of what it means to avoid making mistakes. For Napoleon, it is clear that errors cannot be avoided by caution, let alone hesitation. For error is either failure to take advantage of an opportunity or to offer an opportunity to one's enemy. As Napoleon, Patton, and all significant leaders have understood, opportunity is the fulcrum on which one rises to victory or falls to defeat. Errors are either failures to act or actions that provide advantage to your competition. The vaccine against error understood this way is not caution, but daring.

5. Leadership Is Supple

A leader is a man who can adapt principles to circumstances.

This definition, written on one of the index cards on which Patton habitually typed notes from his extensive reading in military history and military science, is highly instructive. The key is the word *adapt.* What we *expect* here is the word *apply.* But Patton was too aggressive and too original to content himself with the mere application of principles to circumstances. Something more basic and more active was required. As he saw it, principles were important, but the exigencies of present circumstances were even more critical. In confronting reality, the object is not to forget or abandon principles, but to allow them to be transformed by the demands of the moment.

Put another way, leadership is a synthesis of theory and practice, of preparation and spontaneity, of rehearsal and improvisation.

6. Leadership Is Not a Popularity Contest

Goddammit, I'm not running for Shah of Persia. There are no practice games in life. It's eat or be eaten, kill or be killed. I want my bunch to get in there first, to be the "fustest with the mostest." They won't do it if I ask them kindly. That was the only mistake Robert E. Lee ever made. He gave suggestions instead of orders and it cost him the war.

Don't confuse leadership with a popularity contest. Focus on the mission and on getting your people to focus on the mission.

7. Always Lead from the Front

You young lieutenants have to realize that your platoon is like a piece of spaghetti. You can't push it. You've got to get out in front and pull it.

A leader leads from the front, not from behind. She takes the risks she asks others to take. She sets the example for others to follow.

8. Dominate, but Never Domineer

In dominating, he did not domineer. Patton always led his men. He did not rule them.

—Robert Allen, *Lucky Forward*

Leadership is about maintaining a delicate balance between pushing and guiding. The genuine leader leads. He mentors. He guides. He sets examples. He mediates, and he adjudicates. He makes decisions. But, whatever else he does, he does not *merely* command.

9. The Most Important Task of Every Commander

Does not make any difference what the rank is for promotion. Could be for a colonel or corporal. Picking the right leader is the most important task of every commander. When I have a promotion to make, I line up all of the candidates and give them a problem I want them to solve. I say, "Men, I want a trench dug behind a warehouse. Make this trench eight feet long, three feet wide, and six inches deep." That's all I tell them. I use some warehouse that has windows or a large knot hole. While the candidates are checking out the tools they want to use, I get inside the building and watch through the window or knot hole. The men will drop all of the spades and picks on the ground behind the warehouse as I watch. After resting for several minutes, they will start talking about why I want such a shallow trench. They will argue that six inches is not deep enough for a gun emplacement. Others will argue that such a trench should be dug with power equipment. Others will say it is too hot or too cold to dig. If the men are officers there will be complaints that they should not be doing such lowly labor as digging a trench. Finally, one man will give an order to the others, "Let's get this trench dug and get out of here.

Doesn't make any difference what that old SOB wants to do with the trench."

That man gets the promotion. Never pick a man because he slobbers all over you with kind words. Too many commanders pick dummies to serve on their staff. Such dummies don't know how to do anything except say, "Yes." Such men are not leaders. Any man who picks a dummy cannot be a leader. Pick the man that can get the job done!

An effective manager not only knows how to delegate tasks, but knows how to delegate leadership as well. Read Patton's remarks carefully. The primary criterion a leader should meet is the ability to get the job done, whatever it may be. Observe candidates for promotion *in action*. Evaluate the results. Focus on the individuals who habitually cut to the chase and are able to marshal people and resources to get the job done.

10. Selecting Leaders

Select leaders for accomplishment and not for affection.

Do not confuse loyalty with friendship. In any enterprise, loyalty must be based on achievement. It is certainly possible to like someone who just isn't very good at his or her job. That's fine. Just don't let your affection influence your choice of leadership. Evaluate achievement and base your staffing and promotion decisions on that. By the same token, do not prevail on your friendship with a boss to secure promotion for yourself. Bosses come and go. Build your career on a permanent record of accomplishment.

11. There Can Be No Halfway Leaders

A general who had been relieved came in at his own request and tried to explain why he was no good. I offered him a lesser command in another division, but he told me he needed forty-eight hours to consider it. I did not tell him so, but I realized that any man who could not make up his mind in less than forty-eight hours was not fit to command troops in battle.

The point here is not that Patton valued snap judgments, but that he believed the truly important decisions—those involving core values—did not require much time for thought. The answers to such issues should be second nature, a part of the man.

This quotation also makes clear that Patton firmly and intuitively grasped what made a good leader. He did not compromise in this area.

12. Cherish Your Prima Donnas

In my experience, all very successful commanders are prima donnas, and must be so treated. Some officers require urging, others require suggestions, very few have to be restrained.

Most senior managers expect their subordinate managers to "behave like professionals." The fact is, this is often an unrealistic expectation. Most leaders become leaders because they are uncommon—and they *know* it. The debate as to whether leaders are born or made is bogus. The truth is that some leaders are made, but most leaders *make themselves*. How? They believe that they are leaders. They are, in short, prima donnas.

Patton had sufficient insight into himself to recognize that he was a prima donna. (Certainly, none of his fellow officers would deny that he was.) But he also had sufficient judgment to apply this self-assessment to other officers and to accept the same difficult and demanding quality in them.

If you are a senior manager, you should not attempt to transform your prima donnas into "regular guys." You've got all the "regular guys" (and the term is meant to apply to both sexes) that you need. Accept your subordinate managers as prima donnas, if that's what they are, and make the most of it. Appeal to their self-confidence. Appeal to the qualities that convince them they are special. Encourage them to be even more exceptional as leaders, innovators, and doers.

13. The Image of Leadership

Generals must never show doubt, discouragement, or fatigue.

As a leader, you cannot always afford the luxury of revealing all of your feelings, particularly if they are negative. Patton always looked and acted the part of the confident commander. Take another look at that word "acted." Patton believed that a commander had to be, in large part, an actor. He plays the *role* of leader, and in the script for that role there is no room for expressions of doubt, discouragement, or fatigue.

You may have heard that employees enjoy working for a boss who isn't afraid to show his or her "human" or "vulnerable" side. Don't believe it! Even employees who say things like this actually want to take direction from someone they consider infallible, supremely confident, always decisive, and ever energetic. Don't try to avoid your negative feelings, but do keep them away from your subordinates.

14. One of Us

In cold weather, General Officers must be careful not to appear to dress more warmly than the men.

Fighting through the grim winter of 1944, especially during the Battle of the Bulge, and as a student of the disastrous Russian Campaign of Napoleon, General Patton fully understood the physical, emotional, and spiritual toll continuous exposure to cold weather takes. As a leader, it is part of your job to appreciate the toll that difficult times may take on the people you manage. In tough times, under adverse business conditions, your subordinates are likely to assume that you are not suffering and will not suffer as much as they. They may assume, right or not, that they will be fired long before you will. They may assume, right or wrong, that you have some sort of golden parachute and will survive, even prosper, if the worst happens. Effective managers must conduct themselves so that it is clear that they and their subordinates have an equal stake in the fate of the organization. You don't want to appear more comfortable than those who work for you. If employees suspect that they will be sacrificed to you, loyalty, as well as productivity, will disintegrate almost instantly when the chips are down.

15. By Example and Voice

Officers must assert themselves by example and voice.

Act like a leader and speak like a leader. This does not mean shouting your message, but your message must be clear, unmistakable, and always delivered with conviction. When issuing instructions, your sentences should be declarative, not exclamatory and not questioning. You are not only the source of direction for your organization, you are its chief example as well.

16. A Commander Knows!

I can tell a commander by the way he speaks. He does not have to swear as much as I do, but he has to speak so that no one will refuse to follow his order. Certain words will make you sound like a staff officer and not a commander. A good commander will never express an opinion! A commander knows! No one cares what your opinion is! Never use the words, "In my opinion, I believe, I think or I guess," and never say "I don't think!" Every man who hears you speak must know what you want. You can be wrong, but never be in doubt when you speak! Any doubt or fear in your voice and the troops can feel it. Another thing. Never give a command in a sitting position unless you are on a horse or on top of a tank!

You are a manager, not a military commander. But, make no mistake, you need to establish the authority of your directives and instructions. You need to ensure that what you want done *gets done.*

Examine your speech: Do you unnecessarily qualify instructions with the phrases Patton mentions—*In my opinion, I think, I guess,* and the like? Effective managers inspire confidence. This can be accomplished, in part, by making positive, direct, unqualified statements. How can you make such statement? Base what you say on accurate information. Get the facts.

Examine your body language. It is a fact that important instructions and other information are best conveyed from a standing position. This is true even on the phone. The next time you have something really important to say to a client, coworker, subordinate, or boss, even by telephone, say it standing up.

17. Generals Get Shot At

I crossed the bridge over the [Saar] River under alleged fire. It was purely a motion on my part to show the soldiers that generals could get shot at. I was not shot at very much.

Patton was both praised and criticized for exposing himself to enemy fire. He felt that it was essential for a leader to share the responsibilities and the risks of those who are led. How many employees feel that their boss shares their risks? In an age of golden parachutes and the like, probably not many.

Take a closer look at this passage, however. The phrase "alleged fire" and the sentence "I was not shot at very much" are telling. Patton was daring, but not suicidal and never reckless. He assessed the risk (getting shot), weighed it against the reward (creating solidarity with his soldiers), and determined that the risk was manageable and well worth the reward.

18. If You Done It, It Ain't Bragging

Without a solid record of success, Patton's theatrics would have been sheer buffoonery. Dizzy Dean is reputed to have said, "If you done it, it ain't bragging." Patton "done it" over and over again . . . Moreover, he never squandered the lives of his troops needlessly. Patton's sense of what was possible on the battlefield was unequalled. Fiascoes like the Fifth Army's attack on the Rapido River or the First Army's attack in the Hurtgen Forest never occurred under his command. In the Third Army we knew what General Patton expected us to do, and we believed that if we did it we would win. That's what generalship is about.

—GEN. OMAR N. BRADLEY, *A SOLDIER'S STORY*

Patton was an actor, no doubt about it. He believed that a big part of a general's job was to *act* the part of a general. And this is true of any leader. But it is also true that theatrics are hollow in the absence of results. Don't mistake the *show* of leadership, no matter how necessary, for leadership itself. Patton never made that mistake.

19. Fight Bad Orders

We still did not have a single bridge over the Our or the Sauer River and the attack was very sticky. I made an unsuccessful attempt to delay the withdrawal [under orders from higher headquarters] of the 17th Airborne Division. I believe that a good deal of my success and a great deal of my unpopularity is due to the fact that I fought every order to take troops away from me, and frequently succeeded in holding on to them or in getting others to replace them.

A leader must often deal with "enemies" both internal and external. Competition may come from other firms, and it may also come from other departments and other managers who bid for scarce resources. It is generally a good thing to be a team player, but there are limits. Know when to fight for resources and to hold on to the personnel and other resources you need. Corporate politics can be a bloody business indeed.

20. Leadership and Risk

It takes the right mixture of common horse sense and stupidity to make a good commander.

A leader must be intelligent and possessed of sound judgment driven by common sense. However, a leader must be willing to take risks that "smarter" folk might well avoid. A leader cannot be afraid to buck the odds, when need be. Most of all, a leader needs to be "stupid" enough not to give in to his or her fears. As Patton saw it, part of command is an ability to narrow focus, excluding from your field of vision those aspects of reality that would very sensibly create fear in an "average" person. If this is "stupidity," embrace it wholeheartedly.

21. The Extra Mile

Do more than is required of you.

What is the distance between a leader and those who spend their lives and careers merely following?

The extra mile.

Advancement comes with habitually doing more than you are asked.

22. The Leadership Commitment

To command an army well a general must think of nothing else.

—NAPOLEON, QUOTED BY PATTON IN HIS WEST POINT NOTEBOOK

Nine-to-fivers rarely rise above the middling positions in any organization. This does not mean that the successful manager must be a workaholic grind, but it does mean that he or she never truly stops thinking about the job. A genuine career requires a focused commitment of life energy.

3

"Always Attack. Never Surrender."

On Developing a Winning Attitude

*"Americans love to fight.
All real Americans
love the sting of battle."*

23. A Philosophy of Combat

Go forward.

This is the quintessential Patton quotation. In these two words is the heart of his leadership philosophy and his combat strategy. The words do not simply mean "never retreat." Although they do, in part, mean just that. Nor do they simply mean "don't stand still"—although it is also true that Patton repeatedly advised against "digging in." The business of an army is not to dig in and defend territory, he often said, but to move and to destroy the enemy: "We are going to move and move fast!" Patton declared when he was in charge of the Desert Training Center near Indio, California. "We are not going to dig any foxholes and wait for the enemy to come shootin' at us. We will be shootin' at them first! When every soldier can move a mile with his rifle in fifteen minutes, we will confuse the hell out of them. We will be where the enemy never expects us to be!" Later, in North Africa, when Patton saw a group of soldiers digging foxholes, he "told them that if they wanted to save the Graves Registration [personnel] burials that was a fine thing to do."

In its most profound management sense, *Go forward* is a recognition that business, like all aspects of life, is dynamic, not static. To go forward is to make each move, each action, count. To go forward is to give up dwelling on the past.

This does not mean forgetting the past. Patton was an avid reader of history and military history. He referred to himself as a "profound student of history" and frequently quoted the likes of Caesar, Napoleon, and Clausewitz by heart. In fact, Patton often observed that there were "no new battles to be fought." Nevertheless, technology changes, and new weapons are invented. Part of *going forward* is to evaluate and embrace new technology. Patton was trained as a cavalryman. As a young officer, he became an Olympic-class expert with the saber and was appointed the U.S. Army's first Master of the Sword. He even helped design a new saber for military use. No military vehicle is older than the horse, and no weapon more traditional than the saber. Yet, in World War I, Patton became a pioneer in the development of that odd-looking new weapon called the tank. And even while commanding tanks in World War II, he advised certain promising junior armor officers to leave the tank corps and take flight training, because, he observed, the future of war was in the air.

Yet, Patton also insisted, there were no new battles. The job of an effective general was to commit history's key battles to memory and apply their lessons to present situations.

Apply is the important word. Use the past to *go forward.* Experience and a knowledge of the past are useful to a manager insofar as they can be applied to the present and to the future.

24. We Will Win

We will win because we will never lose! There can never be defeat if a man refuses to accept defeat. Wars are lost in the mind before they are lost on the ground. No nation was ever defeated until the people were willing to accept defeat.

Success is an attitude. True, success at any given moment may be measured by sales figures, revenue, profits, production numbers—whatever. But success, in the long run, is an attitude. It is a winning attitude that motivates success, and it is a winning attitude that sustains success.

It is easy to know when you have won. Just declare a victory.

It is just as easy to know when you're defeated. Give up.

Expect reverses. Expect losses. They are inevitable. But why give them the last word? Take them as bumps along the road to victory.

25. Work on a Superiority Complex

We must have a superiority complex. Always attack. Never surrender.

—MESSAGE TO OFFICERS PRIOR TO THE OPERATION TORCH LANDINGS IN NORTH AFRICA, NOVEMBER 1942

Most of us have been raised to be modest, to avoid inflated self-assessment. Most of us have learned this lesson all too well and tend, therefore, to underestimate what we are capable of. Furthermore, put in the position of managing others, we project that underestimate on them. We undervalue their potential as well.

Patton was well aware of this tendency, and he directed his officers to guard against it. Why accept a self-diagnosed "inferiority complex"? What does it gain us? If we are going to diagnose our mental state, why not bestow upon ourselves a *superiority complex*? At least this self-appraisal has a chance of producing the results we want.

26. Be a Steamroller

Have been giving everyone a simplified directive of war. Use steamroller strategy; that is, make up your mind on course and direction of action, and stick to it. But in tactics, do not steamroller. Attack weakness.

—LETTER FROM NORTH AFRICA, NOVEMBER 2, 1942

Recognize the difference between strategy and tactics. Strategy is an overall, big-picture plan, which includes a set of goals. Tactics are the means by which you intend to carry out your strategy. Tactics include objectives, which are steps toward goals. Patton advised steadfastness in setting overall strategy, but flexibility in creating tactics. This kind of double-barreled leadership approach will help ensure that your organization has consistency of purpose and direction, yet retains the flexibility to respond to problems and crises and to exploit opportunities when they arise.

27. Keep Moving

You keep moving and the enemy cannot hit you.
When you dig a foxhole, you dig your grave.

The winning attitude is one of movement and progress, not digging in and holding ground. Defensive postures are illusions. Digging in may make you *feel* safe, but, in reality, you have transformed yourself into a stationary target. In any competitive enterprise, action is preferable to inaction.

28. When In Doubt, Attack

Wars are not won by defensive tactics.

Patton was fond of saying, "When in doubt, attack."

> *The trick expression, "Dig or die," is much overused and much misunderstood. Wars are not won by defensive tactics. Digging is primarily defensive. The only time it is proper for a soldier to dig is when he has reached his final objective in an attack, or when he is bivouacking under circumstances where he thinks he may be strafed from the air or is within artillery range of the enemy. Personally, I am opposed to digging under such circumstances, as the chance of getting killed while sleeping normally on the ground is quite remote, and the fatigue from digging innumerable slit trenches is avoided. Also, the psychological effect on the soldier is bad, because if he thinks he has to dig he must think the enemy is dangerous, which he usually is not.*
>
> *"Hit the dirt" is another expression which has done much to increase our casualties. Frequently in fighting the Germans, and probably other troops in the next war, we will find that they have resort to their knowledge of our custom of hitting the dirt. What they do is wait until we have arrived at a predetermined spot on which they have ranged rockets, mortars, or artillery, and then they put on a sudden and violent machine-gun fire—frequently straight up in the air. The soldier, obsessed with the idea of hitting the dirt, lies down and waits supinely for the arrival of the shells . . . He usually doesn't have to wait long.*

As an alternative to "dangerous" defensive tactics, Patton advocated "marching fire":

> *. . . keep moving. This fire can be delivered from the shoulder, but it is just as effective if delivered with the butt of the rifle halfway between the belt and the armpit. One round should be fired every two or three paces. The whistle of the bullets, the scream of the ricochet, and the dust, twigs, and branches which are knocked from the ground and the trees have such an effect on the enemy that his small-arms fire becomes negligible. . . . Keep walking forward. Furthermore, the fact that you are shooting adds to your self-confidence, because you feel that you are doing something, and are not sitting like a duck in a bathtub being shot at.*

Too many CEOs and managers take a defensive approach to business. Patton would point out to them that they are transforming themselves into sitting ducks by making themselves predictable. As the cliché goes, the best defense is a good offense. Go forward. Be aggressive. Don't give your competition a chance to pin you down. Trepidation and loss of morale come with a defensive posture. Attack the problem, attack the market, attack the competition, and you are proceeding positively. Fear will melt, and morale will rise.

29. Reject Foolish Consistency

During our operation in Tunisia, we were under very close tutelage by the British, and I had a British Brigadier General at my Headquarters. Sometime around the beginning of the second week of April, I was making desperate efforts to take the mountain called Djebel Berda. After supper on this particular evening, General Eddy, commanding the 9th Division, which was conducting the attack, came to my quarters, and in the presence of the English Brigadier stated that, while he would carry out my orders of continuing the attack, he felt that it was hopeless, owing to the fact that the infantry regiments engaged in it had already suffered twenty-six percent casualties.

I was faced with the necessity of making a decision either to continue a hopeless attack or to lose face in front of the British and violate my own principles of war by agreeing to stop the attack. I felt that, under the circumstances, I was not justified in demanding further sacrifice. I therefore directed General Eddy to discontinue the attack. I think this was one of the most difficult decisions I ever had to make.

Fortunately, on the next day, the 1st Division across the valley captured an Observation Post from which we could place a very effective artillery concentration on the part of the mountain we had been trying to storm. We put all the guns in the corps and the two divisions on the target and gave them, just at dawn, twenty-five rounds per gun of rapid fire with white phosphorus, with the idea of persuading the enemy that we were going to launch an attack and hoping he would man his trenches. After a wait of ten minutes, we put on a second twenty-five rounds per gun of high explosive. As a result of this operation, we took the position without casualty, except to the Germans.

Critics of Patton have always been quick to accuse him of inflexibly holding to his "always attack" maxim, regardless of costs. It is true that he clung to this idea fiercely, but never foolishly. Doubtless it was a difficult decision to break off an attack, but, convinced that it was necessary to do so, Patton willingly accepted what he saw as loss of face in order to avoid useless loss of life.

"A foolish consistency," Ralph Waldo Emerson wrote, "is the hobgoblin of little minds." All managers would do well to link this statement with Patton's words on the Tunisian campaign and remember both when they are tempted to act in blind obedience to an inflexible principle.

30. When Necessary, Question Your Orders

On the fourteenth of July [1943, during the Allied invasion of Sicily], I received a telegram from [British] General [Harold] Alexander [commander of the Fifteenth Army Group, to which Patton's command was subject] to the effect that I would take up a defensive position in the vicinity of Caltanissetta to cover the left rear of the British Eighth Army. To have adhered to this order would have been disloyal to the American Army. With the help of General Keyes, General Wedemeyer, and General Gay, I drafted an order for an enveloping attack, via Agrigento and Castelvetrano, on Palermo.

Accompanied by General Wedemeyer, I then flew to Africa and presented this order to General Alexander, stating that I was convinced that this was what he intended, and not that I should remain in a defensive attitude. I asked him to initial the order. He did so, but stated I should not attack Agrigento unless I could do so with a reconnaissance in force [that is, a small force]. I did it with a reconnaissance in force, using all the troops I had available—namely, the 3d Division, part of the 82d Airborne, two Ranger Battalions, and a task force of the 2d Armored.

Had I failed, I would have been relieved. We took Palermo on the twenty-second.

This is one of the most famous and daring of Patton's exploits. Believing it would be a betrayal ("disloyal") of the American army to relegate it to a defensive role in a *British* invasion of Sicily, he bent and then broke the orders of the British overall commander to whom he was subordinate, first persuading General Alexander to allow him to attack Agrigento, albeit with a small "reconnaissance in force," then, on his own, redefining "reconnaissance in force" as "all the troops I had available"! As it turned out, Patton's operation was a resounding success, resulting in the fall of Palermo, Sicily's major city.

But is this a sound lesson for managers? After all, as Patton correctly observes, if he had failed, he would have been fired.

Perhaps the real lesson here is not necessarily to disobey orders, but to question them when necessary and then always to act with a keen awareness of what is at stake. If the price of failure is high, the value of what is to be gained better be much higher. (As Patton saw it, the prize was not only Palermo, but the honor, morale, and future efficacy of the U.S. Army.) The reward must greatly outweigh the risk. And the leader must fully understand and accept the risk.

31. We're Not Holding Anything!

There's another thing I want you to remember. Forget this goddamn business of worrying about our flanks, but not to the extent we don't do anything else. Some goddamned fool once said that flanks must be secured and since then sons of bitches all over the world have been going crazy guarding their flanks. We don't want any of that in the Third Army. Flanks are something for the enemy to worry about, not us. I don't want to get any messages saying that, "We are holding our position." We're not holding anything! Let the Hun do that. We are advancing constantly and we're not interested in holding on to anything except the enemy. We're going to hold on to him by the nose and we're going to kick him in the ass; we're going the kick the hell out of him all the time and we're going to go through him like crap through a goose . . . We have one motto, "L'audace, l'audace, toujours l'audace!" Remember that, gentlemen.

Sometimes a leader needs to shake his organization into taking a fresh look at mission and methods. All military commanders are indoctrinated in the necessity of guarding one's flanks—the vulnerable sides of an advancing column of troops. This often necessitates taking up a series of defensive positions. For the invasion of Europe, Patton was determined to change the focus of the Third Army to achieve a singular goal: advance. He crystallized this in a favorite quotation from Frederick the Great of Prussia: "Audacity, audacity, always audacity!"

While some did and may still disagree with Patton's methods and even deplore some aspects of his personality, no one can argue with the results he achieved in the European theater of war, and, certainly, no one can deny that each and every man in the Third Army understood his organization's goals.

32. Up the Ante

[General Omar] Bradley called up to ask me how soon I could go on the defensive. I told him I was the oldest leader in age and in combat experience in the United States Army in Europe, and that if I had to go on the defensive I would ask to be relieved. He stated I owed too much to the troops and would have to stay on. I replied that a great deal was owed to me, and unless I could continue attacking I would have to be relieved.

One of Patton's unswerving principles was to attack, not to defend. This was especially true when the Germans were in full retreat in the waning weeks of the war. Asked to assume a defensive role, Patton laid everything on the line.

Is this a useful example of leadership? Risking a career for the sake of a principle?

Each manager must decide that for himself. To Patton, however, the issue was not subject to question.

33. Better to Attack with What You Have

On December 19, 1944, General Eisenhower had a meeting at Verdun with General Bradley, General Devers, and myself and the members of his Staff present. The decision was made for the Third Army to attack the southern flank of the Bulge. I was asked when I could make the attack. I stated that I could do so with three divisions on the morning of the twenty-third of December. I had made this estimate before going to Verdun, and had taken exactly eighteen minutes to make it. General Eisenhower stated that I should wait until I got at least six divisions. I told him that, in my opinion, a prompt attack with three was better than waiting for six—particularly when I did not know where I could get the other three. Actually the attack of the III Corps with the 80th, 26th, and 4th Armored Divisions jumped off on the morning of December 22, one day ahead of the time predicted.

In making this attack, we were wholly ignorant of what was ahead of us, but were determined to strike through to Bastogne, which we did on the twenty-sixth. I am sure that this early attack was of material assistance in producing our victory.

The Battle of the Bulge was the last major German offensive of World War II, and it caught the Allied forces off-guard, completely surrounding the 101st Airborne and elements of other units. The Allies had generally assumed that the Germans had been defeated, that the war was drawing to a close. Patton and others understood, however, that if the German all-or-nothing offensive succeeded, the war would be prolonged at very great cost. Pushing back the offensive and rescuing the surrounded 101st required immediate action, Patton believed, and he could not wait for ideal conditions. Leadership is often a matter of balancing timing against available resources. Opportunities are easily lost while waiting for "perfect" conditions.

34. The Danger of Caution

I felt that, with our entry into Bastogne, the German was licked, and that it was not necessary to hold a reserve, but to attack with everything we had.

—PATTON ON THE CONCLUDING PORTION OF THE BATTLE OF THE BULGE

Is it possible to be overly prudent? Patton knew this to be the case. Caution can result in lost opportunity, which, in war as in business, can have devastating consequences. An effective leader continually assesses risks versus rewards and is willing to gamble—when he is convinced that he has a sure thing.

35. Determination

Patton ordered that the Third Army would continue its advance across France during August–September 1945, no matter what. When the tanks started running out of gas, one tank would drain the fuel from the rest in its platoon, and when that tank ran out of gas, the crew was to get out and walk.

A large part of leadership is stubborn determination, a certain single-mindedness. If you want progress, you must rule out all the excuses that impede progress. Patton focused on advancing across Europe and would accept no excuse for hesitation or delay.

36. A Simple Plan of Attack

Hold the enemy by the nose and kick him in the pants.

This is a favorite Patton maxim, frequently quoted by the general's admirers, colleagues, and subordinates. He explained it this way:

> *The policy of holding the enemy by the nose with fire and kicking him in the pants with movement is just as true as when I wrote it, some twenty years ago [about 1925], and at that time it had been true since the beginning of war. Any operation, reduced to its primary characteristics consists in moving down the road until you bump into the enemy. It may be one road or it may be several roads. When you have bumped, hold him at the point of contact with fire with about a third of your command. Move the rest in a wide envelopment so that you can attack him from his rear flank. The enveloping attack should start first. The initial nose attack starts to move forward only when the enemy has properly reacted to the enveloping attack. Then the direct attack can go in easily and fast.*

There are at least two major lessons in this quotation. The first is simply to avoid blundering into "battle"—whether that battle is a major project, a major client presentation, or a real fight. Do what you must to take complete control of the situation. In the case of attacking an actual enemy, Patton's strategy was to occupy and hold him with fire from the front, while the bulk of his forces (two-thirds) marched around the enemy's rear flank (the vulnerable side toward the rear of the enemy forces) to envelop (surround) him. This tactic applies not only to combat. You can use it to manage

Patton as cadet adjutant at the U.S. Military Academy, West Point, 1909, the year of his graduation.

Lt. Col. Patton in France during World War I, summer of 1918, standing in front of a French Renault tank.

Maj. Gen. Patton addressing of the 4th Division rally in the Fourth Corps Area, May 1941, at Fort Benning, Georgia.

Patton during Louisiana Maneuvers, 1941, with Col. Harry A. Flint and Brig. Gen. Geoffrey Keyes.

Patton, commander 2nd Armored Division, and Lt. Col. R. W. Grow confer at Manchester Tennessee June 19, 1941.

Patton reads a compass in front of an M3 light tank at the Desert Training Center, California.

With President Franklin D. Roosevelt in Casablanca, North Africa, January 17, 1943.

Patton decorating 1st Lt. Leon Goralins, Chaplain 213th 1st Armored Division C.A., with the Silver Star.

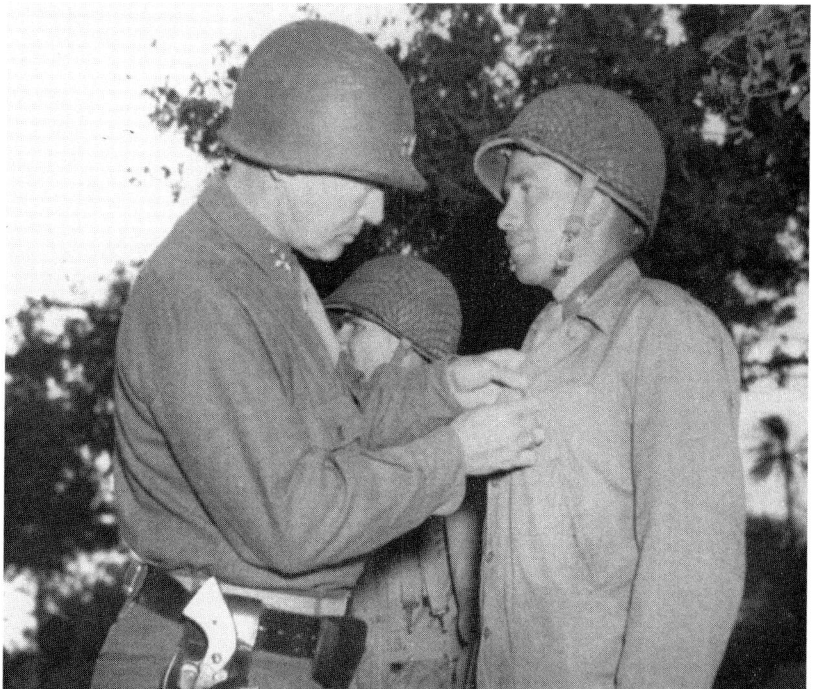

Patton during the Sicily invasion: looking over the town of Gela, July 11, 1943.

Patton, 7th Army commander, discusses the capture of Palermo with his staff, July 23, 1943.

Patton in Sicily, July 11, 1943. The general walks on a mat laid on the sandy beach to facilitate motor transport.

Patton in a tactical conference with General G. K. Roosevelt, Sicily, August 4, 1943.

any high-stakes situation. Deploy your resources so that you can take control of the situation and *work the problem* rather than allow the problem to work *you.* Envelop the situation. Surround it. Manage it.

And there is a second lesson to be learned here. Compare Patton's statement of tactics—*Hold the enemy by the nose and kick him in the pants*—and the straightforward paragraph in which he elaborates on it with the typical tome on business strategy or even the typical "mission statement" of the typical business. Where these rattle and creak with empty jargon, and plenty of it, Patton expresses his guiding tactic in a vivid image and with the most direct language possible. It is not just that he was a good writer (and he was!), but that he understood, to the soles of his boots, who he was and what he was supposed to do.

Patton's statement is simple. All statements of mission and tactics should be simple—even in as complex an enterprise as war or business. But such statements can be simple only if the manager thoroughly understands his or her mission, his or her purpose, his or her objectives, and his or her goals. Do you want to test your understanding of these things? Begin by trying to put them into words as simple, as succinct, and as vivid as those of General Patton. If those words keep coming out like MBA-style gobbledegook, rethink and rethink again what you are about until you can express it with the equivalent of *Hold the enemy by the nose and kick him in the pants.*

37. Defeat Is Self-Defeat

YOU ARE NOT BEATEN UNTIL
YOU ADMIT IT. Hence DON'T.

—INSCRIBED IN PATTON'S FIELD NOTEBOOK

Unfortunately, you will probably never lack for naysayers to tell you that all is lost or that you are beaten. Why join that chorus? Exhaust all alternatives. Victory and defeat are rarely absolutes. There is a whole spectrum of degree between these two extremes. Don't be in a hurry to call that gray area black. You gain nothing by speeding to such a conclusion.

4

"How Do We Know That?"

On Fact Finding, Preparation, and Planning

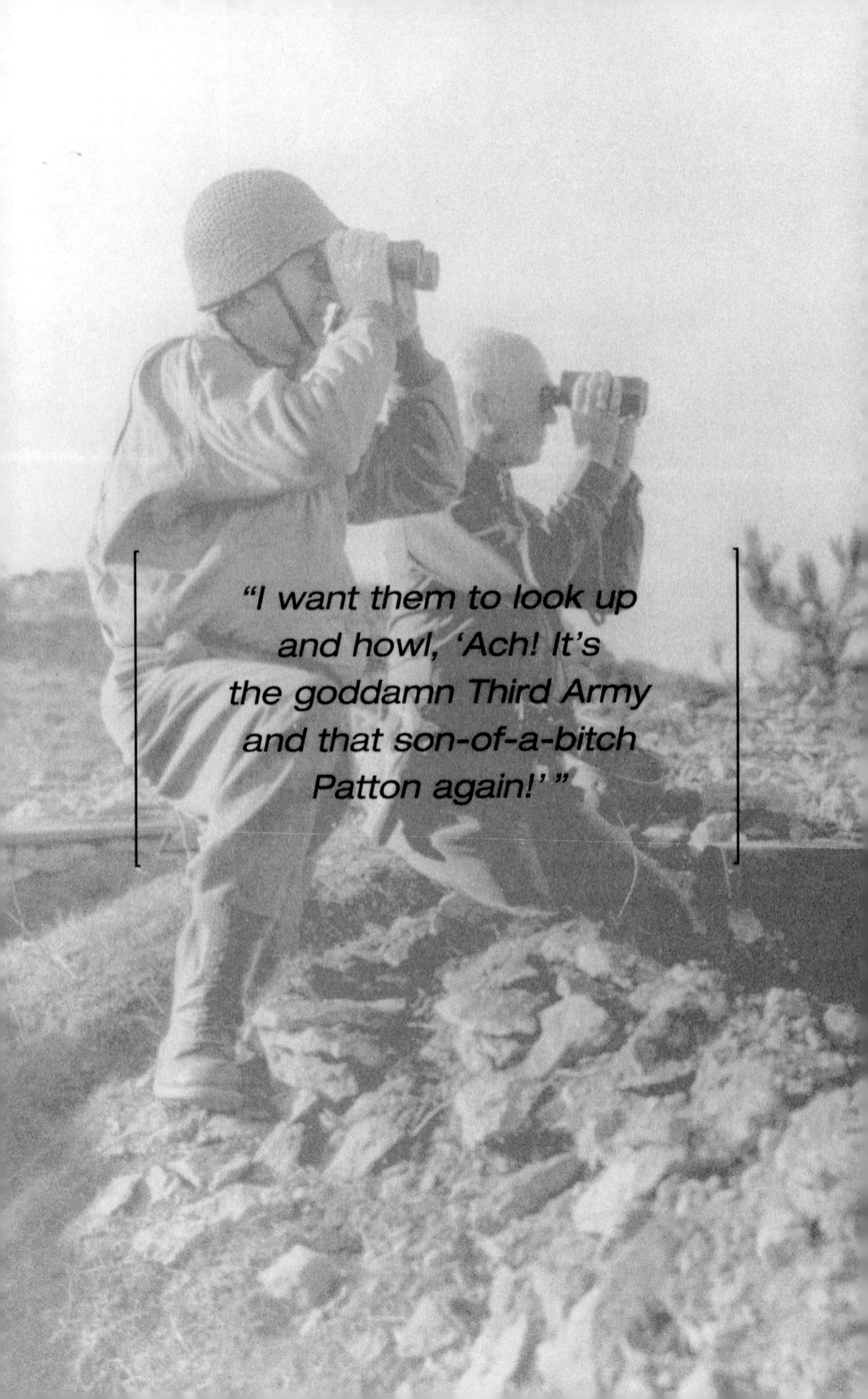

"I want them to look up and howl, 'Ach! It's the goddamn Third Army and that son-of-a-bitch Patton again!'"

38. Strategy and Tactics: Know the Menu

Strategy and tactics do not change. Only the means of applying them are different.

Faced with the task of planning a course of action, it is easy to get overwhelmed by the decisions to be made. Just bear in mind that, in any field, the menu of available strategies and tactics is usually rather limited and can be mastered reasonably well. All that is really subject to change in variety are the technological means of executing choices selected from this menu. A leader must be able to make the connection between the stock of available strategies and tactics and the best, most efficient means currently available for execution.

39. Hit the Books

The only right way of learning the science of war is to read and reread the campaigns of the great captains.

—NAPOLEON, QUOTED BY PATTON IN HIS READING NOTES.

Patton added to this quotation a comment of his own: "And think about what you read."

Those who knew Patton universally described him as "one of a kind" and "an original." Yet he was also the product of his extensive reading of precisely who Napoleon recommended: the great captains. Colleagues and subordinates alike were amazed by Patton's ability to recall the strategic and tactical circumstances of history's great battles.

Patton believed that there were really no new battles—that, in the course of history, essentially all battle types had been fought at one time or another. He considered it a prime responsibility of a general to know the great battles by heart and apply them appropriately.

It behooves any leader to know the history of his or her discipline and to read all the experts in the field, particularly experts whose knowledge is based on actual experience. The object is not to follow any example or method slavishly, but to develop a strategic and tactical vocabulary that will create solutions faster and more efficiently than having to reinvent the wheel with each problem that is encountered.

40. Know Exactly What You Are Doing

There is a time to take counsel of fear, and there is a time to forget your fears. It is always important to know exactly what you are doing. The time to take counsel of your fears is before you make an important battle decision. That is the time to listen to every fear you can imagine! When you have collected all of the facts and fears, make your decision. After you make your decision, forget all of your fears and go full steam ahead.

Patton has often been wrongly accused of acting recklessly. Quite the contrary, he was a careful planner. But once the plans had been formulated, his belief was in ruthless, unremitting, and swift execution. Plan carefully. Inventory everything that can go wrong. Do not be blindly optimistic. Face reality, and plan for reality. The name of the game is contingency. But once the contingencies have been addressed and the plans formulated, push ahead without self-doubt or fear—or, more accurately, without taking counsel of your self-doubt and fear.

"The person who cannot face a fear," Patton said, "will always be running away from it." Better to run toward a goal than away from a fear.

"After you make a decision, do it like hell—and never take counsel of your fears." ("Do not take counsel of your fears" was one of Patton's favorite sayings, but it was not original with him. Patton borrowed the phrase from the great Confederate general Thomas "Stonewall" Jackson.)

41. Use All Available Talent

Patton never launched a campaign without first thoroughly exploring it with his senior commanders. He never jammed an operation down their throats. It was his practice to assemble the corps commanders in the War Room, have the planning group outline a proposed operation, and then invite the former to "work it over." He encouraged free and frank discussion.

—Robert S. Allen, *Drive to Victory*

Surround yourself with people whose knowledge and judgment you trust, then make good use of them. With considerable justification, many managers hesitate to make decisions by committee. In such situations, they believe, bucks get passed and nothing creative ever gets done, or, at least, never gets done in time.

It is all too true that many organizations are addicted to meetings, endless debates that substitute for action. This is frustrating and destructive, to be sure, but so is going to the other extreme, of shunning the counsel of others. Not only do you deprive yourself and your organization of brainpower, you progressively alienate your staff.

Effective leadership is consultative. It welcomes and actively seeks multiple perspectives on any given problem. It does not squander, but rather leverages all available brainpower.

42. Demand Difference of Opinion

No one is thinking if everyone is thinking alike.

Consensus is about everyone acting toward a common purpose. It does not require thinking in lockstep. Leadership requires marshaling resources cooperatively toward a goal while simultaneously preserving—and encouraging—independence of thought. The more minds at work independently on a situation, the better. Encourage the exercise of imagination. Insist on cooperation, but welcome creative dissent. Never close yourself to suggestion and insight from others, including from the most junior members of the team.

43. Always Have a Plan B

We never prepared any battle plan without at least one alternate plan.

—LT. PORTER B. WILLIAMSON,
RECALLING PATTON'S LEADERSHIP STYLE

While Patton believed in committing to an all-out effort once a decision had been made, he also always held something in reserve, not necessarily troops or materiel, but a plan, and maybe two or three.

Effective leadership is multidimensional. That is the nature of the world we live and work in. Formulating a single plan and sticking to it, no matter what, is one-dimensional thinking. To survive and succeed in the multidimensional world, you need more than one plan.

44. Leave Yourself in the Best Possible Position

Never halt on the near side of a river or mountain range. Secure a bridgehead in both cases, because, even if you do not intend to exploit the crossing, the possession of a bridgehead on the far side cramps the enemy's style.

Whatever you do, endeavor to leave yourself in the most favorable position—and put your competition in the least favorable. Here Patton advises making every move count. Even if you don't have as your objective the taking of a bridgehead on the opposite river bank, take the bridgehead nevertheless. It will help secure your position, and it will put the enemy at a disadvantage. Do not become so narrowly focused on a stated objective that you pass up opportunities encountered along the way. Moreover, create sufficiently ambitious objectives in the first place. Ensure that they don't leave a job partially done. Be thorough in framing objectives. The effective manager misses no opportunity and is never too narrowly focused to be thorough.

45. Achieve Speed Without Haste

A pint of sweat will save a gallon of blood.

Patton was so decisive and so vigorously heeded his own advice to *go forward* that he was often accused of acting in haste. "*Haste and Speed:* There is a great difference between these two words," Patton wrote.

> *Haste exists when troops are committed without proper reconnaissance, without the arrangement for proper supporting fire, and before every available man has been brought up. The result of such an attack will be to get the troops into action early, but to complete the action very slowly.*
>
> *Speed is acquired by making the necessary reconnaissance, providing the proper artillery and other tactical support, including air support, bringing up every man, and then launching the attack with a predetermined plan so that the time under fire will be reduced to the minimum. At the battalion level four hours spent in preparation for an attack will probably insure the time under fire not exceeding thirty minutes. One hour spent in preparation of an attack will almost certainly insure time under fire lasting many hours with bloody casualties.*

During the thick of Patton's campaign in Europe, as he drove his troops across France and into Germany, it was reported by an often-hostile press that Patton had earned his nickname "Blood and Guts" by prodigally spilling the blood of his troops. This was absolutely untrue. What Patton extracted from his troops, without stint, was sweat, not blood. He saw training—the sweat—as the means of making his army more efficient and of saving lives.

Lt. Porter B. Williamson recalls that General George C. Marshall, the army's chief of staff, called Patton from Washington.

> *Gen. Patton took the call in front of the staff. We could hear one side of the conversation, "It takes at least six weeks to get a man ready to fight in the desert. Anything short of six weeks, and we will lose more men from heat than from the enemy. George, we must give these men more training!" . . .*
>
> *Gen. Patton did not know and would not accept any half-way measures. No soldier could be "half-way" ready to kill the enemy. He wanted the troops fully trained physically and mentally . . .*
>
> *"It's a damn waste of the most wonderful manhood of America to send green troops into combat before they are ready. We must train to win."*

Fortunately, General Marshall was a wise man, who allowed himself to be persuaded by Patton's argument. Unfortunately, many managers work in environments where wisdom is in short supply. Under pressure from shareholders, upper management demands "results"—perhaps in the form of a product launch before all the groundwork has been laid. Haste is mistaken for speed, and while lives may not be lost if a product is launched prematurely, dollars are squandered and, all too often, careers are short-circuited as well.

Go forward. Move quickly. But go forward and move quickly *first* with all the preparation necessary to ensure an efficient and profitable result, not just a wasteful flurry of action for the appeasement of upper management.

46. Use What Works

One must choose a system and stick to it.

Flexible response is an important quality in any organization. Circumstances are rarely static for long. Failure to respond to change—or, more important, failure to anticipate change—is usually costly and often catastrophic. However, beware of changing procedures arbitrarily. Invest time and effort in determining the most efficient ways of accomplishing routine tasks. Establish these methods as standard. Then do everything within reason to stick to the systems you establish. Once systems are in place, the best policy is to keep the focus on results rather than methods. Life and business are confusing enough without adding into the mix change for its own sake.

47. If It Ain't Broke . . .

In the old Navy of sail there was a custom that the new Officer of the Deck did not call for any change in the setting of the sails for one half hour—that is, for one bell after he took over. The same thing might well apply to commanders and staff officers who take over new jobs in war. They should wait at least a week before they make any radical changes, unless and except they are put in to correct a situation which is in a bad way.

Too many new managers are overeager to put their personal stamp on an operation, whether or not the operation will benefit from their personal stamp. Unless you have been called to correct a situation or unless you see that a situation is obviously bad, rein in your ego, at least for a while. Don't make changes for the sake of making changes. Spend some time studying the operation. Preserve as much of the *useful* status quo as possible. In the absence of pressing needs, *phase in* your innovations over time.

48. Get the Facts

No decision is difficult to make if you will get all of the facts.

Patton conducted himself with dash and decisiveness. For this reason, he was often accused of making snap decisions. In fact, he was a stickler for data. He was highly decisive, but he strove to base decisions on accurate information, and he always took great pains to obtain it. Never confuse decisive decision making with hasty guesswork.

49. Know What You Know

We must always know exactly what we know and what we do not know. Never get the two confused! If we get confused over what we know we can cause many men to die.

As Lt. Porter B. Williamson observed, "'How do we know that?' was a frequent question asked by Gen. Patton." Williamson recalls that "Patton demanded that we sort through our known and unknown facts to *know* exactly what we really *knew*."

> *It could be a shipment of new tanks from Detroit. Some officer might say that the tanks were shipped on a certain date because the shipping notice said when they were shipped. Gen. Patton would explain, "That is the paper work on the tanks which some clerk in some office typed. That clerk would not know for sure that the tanks were even loaded on the flat cars! Or they could be loaded and still sitting in some yard waiting to be hooked onto a train."*
>
> *If no one knew where the tanks were, Gen. Patton would advise one of us to get on the telephone and follow up on the tanks every day. Often his briefing would end, "Raise hell if there is any foul-up!"*

If, to Patton's question of "How do we know that?" an officer replied that the "information came from Washington," Patton (Williamson recalls) "would go into one of his short lectures, saying, 'Washington is the most unreliable source of information you could ever use! An officer in a swivel chair in the Pentagon actually *knows* nothing. All that he knows comes from the soldiers in the field. I do not want to come down too hard on these poor souls in the Pentagon, but they know almost nothing from firsthand knowledge. Everything they *know* is secondhand information. All they do is collect paper facts from the field organizations.'"

Patton insisted on basing plans and decisions on facts gathered at firsthand or as close to firsthand as possible. He habitually analyzed situations to determine just what facts would be most useful. For example, he recommended:

> *In order to evaluate properly the effectiveness of enemy fire, more information than that now obtainable on the subject of casualties is necessary. At the present time, we know only the number of casualties and the type of wounds of those reaching the hospitals, but even in their case, we do not know on what part of the battlefield they were wounded. We have no knowledge of how, or where, battle deaths occurred. In collecting wounded, a method should be prescribed which would show that a man was hit in the vicinity of such and such a point. The Graves Registration personnel should state what type of missile caused death. No medical experience is necessary. Anybody who has seen a few wounds can tell a small-arms wound from a fragmentation wound. This information should be made of record. The location of both types of casualties could be secured through the issue of sketch maps to Medical and Graves Registration personnel. The purpose in collecting the foregoing information is that, if we know what causes our casualties and where they occur, we can take steps to avoid them.*

Patton craved firsthand knowledge, but he was careful to define just what facts he needed. For it is all too easy to get buried under a mountain of useless information. He recommended methods and procedures for acquiring the necessary facts. And he concluded by stating just what purpose would be served by acquiring this particular set of facts. This is the correct and most efficient approach to information: Determine what you need to know, determine how to obtain what you need to know, and have a good reason for wanting the information in the first place. Then, and only then, will you truly know what you know and know what you do not know, so that you can base actions, plans, and decisions on a foundation of firm fact.

50. Share Information

No man can do anything without knowing what he is doing. . . . Generals and staff officers don't win wars! Soldiers win wars! The soldier must know what he is doing at all times. He must know the objective.

And who will tell the soldier what the objective is? Ultimately, the general. It is up to the manager to motivate his people, and the most important ingredient in motivation is knowledge of goals, objectives, purpose. Do *not* expect blind obedience. Teamwork is always more effective than (there is no other word for it) slave work. The first step toward building a team is defining objectives and then making those objectives clear to every member of the team. Moreover, communicate those objectives so persuasively that every member of the team will feel that he or she has the *same* stake in attaining the objectives. Communicate. Don't just give pep talks. Communicate facts. Define the mission. Explain why it is important. Get everyone behind it—not in blind obedience, but in fully knowledgeable compliance.

51. Never Assume

One day a colonel was under attack by Gen. Patton for a decision based on the weather. The colonel explained, "General, we cannot predict the weather. We must assume average weather conditions and plan accordingly."

"We never assume anything is average," Gen. Patton said. "If we do any assuming, we will assume the worst weather."

— RECALLED AND QUOTED BY LT. PORTER B. WILLIAMSON

Patton tried never to *assume* anything, but tried, instead, to gather facts and base decisions on them rather than on assumptions. But it is not always possible to base decisions on complete knowledge of all the variables of a situation. In such cases, Patton's policy was to assume a worst-case scenario and prepare for that. The most misleading assumption possible is based on a vague "average," which has the overall effect of denying reality and the more specific effect of canceling out whatever factor is assumed to be average. What, after all, is "average" weather? It is *non*weather. It is a way of avoiding any thought about the weather.

Managers: Beware of all assumptions, and totally avoid any assumption based on an "average."

52. Learn from the Facts

We passed the scene of the tank battle during the initial German breakthrough. I counted over a hundred American armored fighting vehicles along the road, and, as a result, issued an order, subsequently carried out, that every tank should be examined and the direction, caliber, and type of hit which put it out made of record, so that we would have data from which to construct a better tank.

Patton was a great believer in working from facts, and he continually collected data, always with the object of improving performance. Information is all around us, and it is the manager's job to collect what is useful, analyze it, and make profitable use of it. Why rely on secondhand opinion when your experience is so effective a teacher?

53. Consider the Source

There are more tired division commanders than there are tired divisions. Tired officers are always pessimists. Remember this when evaluating reports.

Be sensitive to the emotional state of subordinate managers and supervisors. Just because you are all "in business," don't assume that the reports and other information you receive are objective. Encourage your staff to take care of themselves, to avoid overwork. And take your own advice in this regard.

Know your limits, and know the limits of those with whom you work. You should always be willing to work to these limits, but you must understand that it is unproductive and even destructive routinely to work beyond them.

54. Consider the Circumstances

In war nothing is ever as bad, or as good, as it is reported to Higher Headquarters.

"Any reports which emanate from a unit after dark—that is, where the knowledge has been obtained after dark—should be viewed with skepticism by the next higher unit. Reports by wounded men are always exaggerated and favor the enemy."

Consider the source and circumstances surrounding the information you obtain secondhand. If your marketing people turn in a rosy or a gloomy projection, investigate the information from which *they* are working. Are they in the dark? Similarly, take with a grain of salt the sales forecast you get from the rep who has just returned—wounded—from an unsuccessful call.

The best information is that which you obtain firsthand. As Patton repeatedly advised, urged, and ordered, *visit the front.*

55. Know Your People

Infantry troops can attack continuously for sixty hours. Frequently much time and suffering are saved if they will do so. Beyond sixty hours, it is rather a waste of time, as the men become too fatigued from lack of sleep.

Know the limits of what you can expect from yourself and your subordinates. Be willing to push to those limits, but understand that pushing beyond them is subject to one of the few absolute laws that govern business and other human endeavor: the law of diminishing returns. Pushed beyond their limits, people work inefficiently, poorly, even counterproductively or destructively.

Patton demanded every bit of what his army could give. He trained his officers and men so that the limit of what they could give was pushed higher than they would have imagined possible: *sixty hours of continuous combat!* But, once established, Patton respected that limit. Like a race-car driver, he gave no second thought to pushing all the way to the red line, but he understood that to go beyond it invites a breakdown. Never hesitate to demand the maximum, but understand that it is futile and destructive to demand more.

56. Know About Your Equipment

Every tank and every truck is as different as every man. Make sure every driver knows his tank or truck. He must know exactly how many gallons of gas and oil is needed for a mile and for an hour—and at different speeds and conditions. . . . Wars are won by knowing what we know. We must know exactly what we need for every day. If we try to carry into combat more gas, oil, supply parts, or anything that we do not need, it could lose a war as quickly as letting a soldier carry a pound more than he needs on his back. We must cut to the bone because we are going to travel fast.

Intelligent, effective action is based on *knowledge*. Patton understood that. But he also understood just what "knowledge" means: It is not just knowing, but knowing what you know—and what you don't know. Effective management requires motivating everyone to know his or her job inside and out, to know what can be done and what cannot. The object is to know as much as possible and then also to be fully aware of the things it is not possible to know.

57. Keep Your Mind Open—and Take Notes

Everything that interested [Patton] was painstakingly typed on note cards and suitably annotated with additional ideas and comments.

—CARLO D'ESTE, *PATTON: A GENIUS FOR WAR*

Those who think of Patton as a one-dimensional man of action are always surprised to learn of the depth and breadth of his scholarship. He studied general history and military history avidly and lifelong. Nor did he read passively. Like all successful students, Patton made his own the knowledge he encountered by taking extensive notes and engaging in a commentary dialogue with the authors he read.

58. Face Facts and Be Honest

God is truth, and don't ever forget it!

The truth: reality, the facts, an honest assessment of the situation. These are not always easy to come by, and they are not always easy to confront and deal with. Often, we prefer to tell people—our subordinates, our colleagues, our bosses, and our customers—what we think they want to hear and even what they tell us they want to hear. And like a Band-Aid or an aspirin, such behavior may bring temporary relief. But disaster can be permanent.

The truth will prevail, one way or another, and usually sooner rather than later. It is better to face it *now* and to convince others to do the same.

This is not for the sake of "building character" or maintaining morality. It is a matter of survival. Whether or not you face it, truth will create consequences.

59. Get Out from Behind Your Desk and Into the World

I want you to know that I do not judge the efficiency of an officer by the calluses on his butt.

Patton had no patience with officers wedded to their swivel chairs. For him, a leader was by definition active—personally involved in the front lines, personally monitoring the execution of orders, and taking every opportunity to make himself physically present to the members of his command. Management by remote control is doomed to fail.

60. Managers Should Not Be Invisible

The more senior the officer who appears with a very small unit at the front, the better the effect on the troops. . . . Corps and Army Commanders must make it a point to be physically seen by as many individuals of their command as possible—certainly by all combat soldiers. The best way to do this is to assemble the divisions, either as a whole or in separate pieces, and make a short talk.

It is almost impossible for a manager to remain both aloof and effective. Come down off the mountain as frequently as possible.

61. Firsthand Information Is Always Best

Remember that your primary mission as a leader is to see with your own eyes and to be seen by the troops when engaged in personal reconnaissance.

—PATTON'S LETTER OF INSTRUCTION TO ALL COMMANDERS, THIRD U.S. ARMY

As Patton saw it, a leader cannot lead by remote control, ensconced in an office. An on-site presence is always called for, the object being not only to see the situation for yourself, but to be seen by the people you lead.

Managers Must See and Be Seen

The more senior the officer, the more time he has. Therefore, the senior should go forward to visit the junior rather than call the junior back to see him.

What a refreshing approach to management! Downright revolutionary: The senior supervisor goes forward to visit front-line subordinates on the assumption that the front-line people are busier.

The fact is that if you want your people to maintain maximum productivity, you should go to them rather than call them back to you. This will also give you an opportunity to see how subordinate supervisors are faring on the front lines. Resist the temptation to "pull rank" and summon subordinates away from their work just so that you can stay in your office.

Patton advised one exception to this procedure: "When it is necessary to collect several commanders for the formulation of a coordinated plan . . . the juniors should report to the superior headquarters." Temper all advice, rules of thumb, and rules of procedure with common sense to suit the circumstances of the moment.

63. Know When to Intervene

If, in a unit the size of a division, the attack is not going well four hours after it starts, it is necessary to make a careful personal reconnaissance and see if it may not be necessary to change the emphasis.

In Patton's experience, a major attack should begin to "produce substantial effect" within four hours of commencement. If it does not, "this does not mean that a man should be wobbly about continuing in the face of uncertain victory, but it does mean that, after four hours, one should know whether the thing is going to be a go or not, and if it is not, he should slow up his attack on the old line while implementing it in a new direction."

Consider this combat advice. The effective manager should undertake a project with a firm idea of how much time and resources to invest in a particular approach to it. She should know what to look for after a given amount of time. She should have some standard by which progress can be gauged. If that standard is not met on schedule, she should *personally* investigate in order to find out what's working and what's not working. Based on this "reconnaissance," she should approach the problem in "a new direction."

The important points are to define *staged* objectives and goals, to assess the degree to which they are or are not being achieved by a set time limit, and to take investigative action if the objectives and goals are not achieved on time. Don't necessarily abandon a project because of uncertain results. But do approach the project from an alternative direction.

64. Roll Up Your Sleeves

On the morning of November 9, 1942 [during the U.S. landing at North Africa], I went to the beach at Fedhala accompanied by Lieutenant Stiller, my Aide. The situation we found was very bad. Boats were coming in and not being pushed off after unloading. There was shell fire, and French aviators were strafing the beach. Although they missed it by a considerable distance whenever they strafed, our men would take cover and delay unloading operations, and particularly the unloading of ammunition, which was vitally necessary, as we were fighting a major engagement not more than fifteen hundred yards to the south.

By remaining on the beach and personally helping to push off boats and by not taking shelter when the enemy planes flew over, I believe I had considerable influence in quieting the nerves of the troops and on making the initial landing a success. I stayed on that beach for nearly eighteen hours and was wet all over all of that time. People say that army commanders should not indulge in such practices. My theory is that an army commander does what is necessary to accomplish his mission, and that nearly eighty percent of his mission is to arouse morale in his men.

Patton included this passage in a chapter of his memoirs entitled "Earning My Pay." He explains the chapter title in this way:

> *The responsibilities of an officer are quite analogous to those of a policeman or a fireman. The better he performs his daily tasks, the less frequently does he have to take direct action.*
>
> *Looking back over my rather lengthy military career, I am surprised at the few times when I have, so to speak, earned my pay. Perhaps, however, the fact that I have had to take drastic action so seldom indicates that, in the interim, I did my duty.*
>
> *The . . . episodes [such as the one just described] stand out in my mind as occasions on which my personal intervention had some value.*

Ideally, the manager creates systems that run so smoothly that his personal intervention in crises is never required. But neither war nor business is ideal, and a leader must recognize when such personal intervention is required. Moreover, he must have the courage, energy, and endurance to intervene, no matter how inconvenient and even if such intervention isn't in his job description. The essence of a leader's mission is not to act in accordance with a job description, but to lead, guide, correct, and encourage the human beings he works with.

65. Exhaust All Possibilities – Personally

Officers must not hesitate to lead. Before an attack is declared hopeless, the senior officer must lead an attack in person.

—INSCRIBED IN PATTON'S FIELD NOTEBOOK

Failure is a part of business. It will happen. The worst failures, however, are those we declare without having exhausted all possibilities and alternatives. Do not be in a hurry to write off any enterprise. When something falters, intervene personally.

Too many managers take charge of obviously successful projects. The time to intervene is not when things are going well, but when they are in trouble.

It takes courage and character to engage a faltering project. It takes courage and character to be a leader.

66. Make Common Cause with Those You Lead

All officers, and particularly General Officers, must be vitally interested in everything that interests the soldier. Usually you will gain a great deal of knowledge by being interested, but even if you do not, the fact that you appear interested has a very high morale influence on the soldier.

Perhaps the most consistently underrated commodity in business is small talk. Too many managers dismiss it as a waste of time. But "small talk"—conversation with subordinates that is not exclusively focused on business or on a particular project or task—is vital to creating a bond between the manager and the people he manages. This does *not* mean faking interest or talking down to employees. It means developing a *genuine* interest in the things that interest them. In identifying with your subordinates, you give them what they both want and need: the opportunity for them to identify with you, the person to whom they look for leadership.

67. Details . . .

Use of Sight: The peep [rifle] sight is not adapted to warfare, since it is inefficient in the dark or in bad light. I have met only three or four officers, out of hundreds questioned, who have ever seen a soldier set a sight in battle. . . . Gun Slings: *The same officers whom I questioned on the sight informed me that they had never seen a gun sling used, except on two occasions by snipers, to aid in firing. Therefore, the heavy and expensive leather gun sling should be dispensed with and a cloth sling, used solely for the purpose of carrying the piece, should be substituted.*

Read these opinions on the use of two components of the soldier's most basic weapon in World War II, the M-1 rifle. Both peep sights and leather rifle slings were standard issue in the era and existed by the millions. Performing in the capacity of a vigilant manager, Patton questioned the utility of these two items. He formed an opinion about them, and he based his opinion on questioning the people who actually made use of the tools at issue. Based on his survey of officers' observations, Patton made the recommendations quoted here.

A good manager questions the status quo, always looking for better, more efficient ways of doing the jobs that need to be done. But such questioning is never idle or whimsical, not does it depend on mystical inspiration. The good manager *asks* questions about the tools and procedures routinely employed. He or she asks the people closest to those tools and procedures. It is on the answers to these questions, given by these people, that he or she bases assessments, opinions, and recommendations concerning tools and procedures.

68. . . . Details

Trenchfoot was becoming very acute at this time. . . . A good deal of the fault was due to the officers and non-coms not taking corrective measures. I wrote a personal letter on trenchfoot and the situation improved.

When you see a serious problem, don't just cast blame, tackle it—even if you believe that it is someone else's responsibility. This is a good example of Patton's famous take-charge attitude.

69. . . . And More Details

In wet weather it is vital that dry socks come up for the soldiers daily with rations.

It is for advice such as this that Patton has sometimes been accused of micromanagement. After all, should a general officer, the man in charge of the movement and lives and actions of hundreds of thousands, concern himself with socks?

An effective manager concerns himself with whatever is needed to get the job done. Patton understood that an army moves on its feet. He also understood that wet socks lead to trenchfoot and other conditions that keep a man from marching. "It's a hell of a lot more important to keep your feet clean than it is to brush your teeth!" he declared. "You use your feet all the time to get at the enemy. Keep your feet clean."

Socks are a small and lowly item, but Patton realized that on *dry* socks (and healthy feet), the efficiency of his army depended. To ensure a supply of dry socks was not micromanagement, but management on the highest scale.

Don't equate attention to detail with micromanagement. Identify those details on which the big picture depends, and then make certain that you manage those details.

70. Position Yourself for Knowledge

Always capture the highest terrain feature in your vicinity at once, and stay on it.

This advice is hardly unique to George S. Patton. Since time immemorial, military commanders have advised taking the high ground. The point is to occupy a position that affords maximum visibility and that commands maximum fields of fire. The army that holds the high ground possesses an inestimable advantage.

As a manager, make it your business to identify the "high ground," advance to it, and hold it. This may be a technological advantage, an information advantage, a market advantage, a special relationship with a customer or vendor. Whatever the high ground is for you, make it a top priority to seize and hold it. It is the difference between controlling a market or other situation and relinquishing control to competitors.

71. Exploit Difficulty

The "Fog of war" works both ways. The enemy is as much in the dark as you are. BE BOLD!!!!!

—INSCRIBED IN PATTON'S FIELD NOTEBOOK

The great military theoretician Karl Maria von Clausewitz (1780–1831) wrote about the "fog of war" as the inevitable confusion that accompanies any battle and that renders the clearest plans difficult to execute. A leader of lesser stuff than Patton would be discouraged by the truth of this concept. Patton, however, accepted it as one of the givens of war and, as such, resolved to make use of it.

Remember that the difficulties, limitations, and pitfalls of any enterprise apply equally to all who engage in that enterprise. Often, the margin between winning and losing is defined by how successfully one copes with—and even exploits—these apparently negative factors. Don't make the mistake of thinking that the work of leadership is difficult *only* for you.

72. Choose Your Competition

You have to pick your enemies with as much care as you do your friends!

To General Patton, few things in life were more precious than loyalty, the loyalty of higher commanders as well as subordinates, and the loyalty of friends. He observed: "Friends are great. Just wonderful to have. Friends are like wine—get better with years." And then he continued:

> *But you need good enemies as much as you need good friends. Having the right enemies is more important than having the right friends. Get the right enemies, and you will have the right friends! You always know where your enemies are. Can never be sure about friends. Sad but true, only a few friends will always be loyal. These lukewarm friends cause people to say, "Protect me from my friends; I can take care of my enemies!" God knows we have enough of these lukewarm friends in the service same as in civilian life. Try to get these types to stand for something. Make them put up or shut up. A great number of military officers I know have never stood for anything other than a short arm inspection! We can differ with each other and still be friends. You will not be my friend if you fail to level with me always.*

Yes, it is a fine policy to be courteous and friendly, to try to get along with everyone and alienate no one—just as long as you can always distinguish your solid friends from those who are wishy-washy, indifferent, "lukewarm." Making such judgments is not always easy, Patton understood, so he came to value his enemies. At least you can understand who they are and where they stand:

> *I have enemies, and I want them to stay enemies. They could never be a loyal friend to anything or anybody. I strike at them every chance I can get. It is far better to lose battles with true friends than to win with the enemy. You do not lose a battle when you fight with true friends because you will always be fighting again for the same things. There is no victory when you win with an enemy. That's the reason I have never liked politics and politicians. They are always switching sides—changing bed partners in their politics.*

Patton's advice is not to go out of your way to be hostile, but simply be wary of certain colleagues, subordinates, supervisors, and so-called "allies." Why? Not out of paranoia—a feeling that everyone is out to get you—but from a conviction that, ultimately, you have to rely most on yourself and on your immediate team. If you don't know someone thoroughly, based on the "acid test" of experience under fire, you can't depend on that person. Chances are he or she just won't measure up to you:

> *We dare not be too trusting of friendly troops, whether they are our own or from some foreign country. We must not treat them as we do the enemy, but we must always wait and see how they fight under enemy fire. That is the acid test of a friend and of a soldier. No other military organization is going to fight as hard and as fast as we will fight. We must be prepared to find our flanks exposed because friendly troops will not move as fast as we will move. Until we know how friendly troops will fight, do not count on them to do much more than bring up our mail!*

73. Assert Control from Day One

We will never let the enemy pick the battle site.

Patton believed in fighting on his own terms. "Now and then we could get caught in a trap set by the enemy," he observed, "but not if we are alert. We will always know more about what the enemy is going to do than their own commanders. The secret is to move fast and in a direction the enemy never expects. The chance of taking losses is too great to fight on a battle site which pleases the enemy. This causes the loss of lives of hundreds of fine American young men. We will decide where and when we will kill the enemy."

The effective manager will find many ways to apply this advice in business. Strategically, you may take it as a commandment to *play to your strengths*. Do as much of your business as possible in the areas and markets in which you have the greatest expertise and the most intensive resources. Exploit your strengths and, to the extent that it is possible, avoid your weaknesses. Tactically, this advice is as simple as choosing where to conduct a piece of business. If you are, for example, making a major sales pitch, it is almost certainly preferable to invite the prospect to lunch at a restaurant of your choosing than it is to meet in the prospect's office, where you will be interrupted by routine business and perhaps even sniped at by office naysayers.

74. Be Reliable, Not Predictable

Never attack where the enemy expects you to come.

In war as in business, it is important to be reliable, but never simply predictable. Innovate. Look for new solutions, even if doing so involves some difficulty: "It is much better to go over difficult ground where you are not expected than it is over good ground where you are expected." The well-worn and overused may be easier in the short run, but it rarely represents a worthwhile investment of time and other resources in the long run.

75. See Reality Through the Eyes of Your Competition

I woke up at 0300 on the morning of November 8, 1944, and it was raining very hard. I tried to go to sleep, but finding it impossible, got up and started to read Rommel's book, Infantry Attacks. *By chance I turned to a chapter describing a fight in the rain in September 1914. This was very reassuring because I felt that if the German could do it, I could, so went to sleep and was awakened at 0515 by the artillery preparation.*

This passage is from the outset of the triumphant capture of Metz and the Saar Campaign (November 8–December 8, 1944). Notice that, for Patton, managing the Third Army was a 24-hour-a-day job. Unable to sleep, he did not seek escape in a novel, but in rereading a book on military tactics by one of Germany's greatest commanders, Field Marshal Erwin Rommel. The effective manager immerses herself in her work and reads whatever literature is available in her field.

Another lesson here. Patton eagerly studied his enemy. He read all the great German tacticians. A leader learns everything he can about his competition. Nor is it always necessary to search high and low for "top-secret" information. Do as Patton did: Start with the information that is available to all, in the form of books, magazine articles, and, these days, information on the Internet. Survey the obvious sources first. Often, they will lead to additional sources of information.

76. Your Rivals Offer Opportunities

When the enemy wavers, throw caution to the winds. He may have a reserve that will stop your pursuit, but it cannot restore the battle. A violent pursuit will finish the show. Caution leads to a new battle.

In a competitive situation, be sensitive to the demeanor of your opponent. Look for weakness, and exploit it. Patton was famous for driving his armies beyond what the average commander would consider prudent. When he waded into battle, some called him reckless. Yet what he proved is that aggression applied swiftly, fully, and appropriately created battles of violent but brief duration. The net result: fewer casualties.

Often, the *thoughtless* exercise of caution gives us the illusion of saving resources and reducing risks. Yet undue caution may actually prolong risks and result in unnecessary losses. Recognize opportunity, and seize it.

77. Results Are Judge and Jury

In the long run, it's what we do, not what we say, that will destroy us.

Everybody is familiar with the cliché "Actions speak louder than words." Patton would have disagreed. In his own career, he had suffered because certain of his comments were quoted out of context, deliberately distorted, or, sometimes, reported straight. He didn't make it a habit to tell the public or higher command ("upper management") what they wanted to hear. So, too many times, despite the obvious success of his actions, his words spoke louder—and got him into trouble, even jeopardizing his career.

Patton *was* a good manager, who, like all good managers, understood how important it is to say the right thing. But he also understood that it is even *more* important to *do* the right thing.

Ultimately, our actions are of greater consequence than our words. In critical situations, telling people what they want to hear may provide the illusion of a solution and bring temporary relief. In the long run, however, this approach will not avert disaster. Say what needs to be said, then act accordingly. Temporary discomfort is better than temporary relief—if it averts permanent catastrophe.

5

“Speed – Simplicity – Boldness”

On Execution and Opportunity

"We're advancing constantly and we're not interested in holding onto anything except the enemy."

78. You Cannot Resist Change—Successfully

If the 14th-Century Knight could adapt himself to gunpowder, we should have no fear of oil, grease, and motors.

—SPEECH TO THE PENNSYLVANIA NATIONAL GUARD, 1930, ABOUT INFANTRY AND CAVALRYMEN ADAPTING TO MECHANIZED WARFARE

Charles Darwin explained what happens to animal species that fail to adapt to changing circumstances. They cease to be. Here Patton uses historical precedent to prepare the next generation of soldiers for a new kind of warfare.

You cannot resist change—successfully. Part of a manager's job is to *manage change,* to lead his or her organization through it productively. This often involves addressing the fears of members of your organization. By all means, address those fears, but make it clear that change is a given and cannot be evaded. Rather, it must be used to its fullest advantage.

79. Fit Plans to Circumstances

One does not plan and then try to make circumstances fit those plans. One tries to make plans fit the circumstances. I think the difference between success and failure in high command depends upon the ability, or lack of it, to do just that.

Planning is a vital element of leadership, but so is the flexibility to adapt plans to changing circumstances. Do not abandon a plan in panic, but realize that rigid adherence to a plan that no longer fits circumstances usually brings disaster. Leadership calls for a delicate combination of preparation and spontaneity.

80. Prepare for Your Luck

"Fortune is a woman who must be wooed while she is in the mood."

—Napoleon, quoted by Patton in his reading notes

No good leader disdains luck, chance, and circumstance. But no good leader passively depends on them, either. Part of leadership is becoming sensitive and open to what fortune and circumstance have to offer and taking advantage of these opportunities when they present themselves—not before and, certainly, not after.

81. Don't Be an Old Maid

There is a right time to make every decision. Trying to find the right time is the most important factor for all decisions. It is a mistake to make a decision too early, and it is a mistake to make a decision too late. The biggest mistake is to never make a decision! Every old maid agrees with me!

Some managers are procrastinators, who put off making a decision until circumstances box them in—and until a "decision" becomes easy: they have *no* choice, but must simply respond, for better or worse, to whatever circumstances dictate. Other managers are overanxious and make a decision—*any* decision—as soon as possible, then struggle with the consequences.

Patton believed that "the best policy is to delay the decision as long as possible so that more facts can be collected." But: "when the decision has to be made, we will never hesitate."

82. Whatever You Do, Decide

When a decision has to be made, make it. There is no totally right time for anything.

Every leader has to make one major concession to the real world, and that is simply this: it *is* the real world. In theory and in games, there is a *right* time to decide and take action. In the real world, however, there is no right time. You cannot control everything. Nor can you wait for the roll of the dice to come out just right. Sometimes you have to move with the numbers you have. Make this fundamental pact with reality, or reality will leave you in the dust.

83. It Is Fatal to Wait for Perfection

The best is the enemy of the good. By this I mean that a good plan violently executed now is better than a perfect plan next week. War is a very simple thing, and the determining characteristics are self-confidence, speed, and audacity. None of these things can ever be perfect, but they can be good.

Management theoreticians are business-school professors, not managers. Your job is to manage, not to theorize about perfect solutions. Perfection is too expensive. It costs too much time. If you wait for the perfect plan or for ideal circumstances, opportunity will be lost. Perfection is static. War, life, and business are dynamic and, therefore, imperfect by definition. To act effectively and intelligently not only doesn't require perfection, it is incompatible with perfection.

Do note, however, that Patton never advised *against* careful planning. In fact, he demanded that, in all situations, his officers always prepare a plan and at least one alternate plan, preferably more than one. But none of these plans had to be perfect, and certainly, none depended on perfect circumstances for execution.

84. Seize Opportunity

I maintained my contention that it is better to attack with a small force at once, and attain surprise, than it is to wait and lose it.

—Patton on his quick action in the Battle of the Bulge

There is a razor-thin line between premature action and seizing opportunity. A good leader recognizes that line and sometimes steps right up to it. Whereas ordinary commanders weighed their resources (numbers of men, amount of supplies) against that of the enemy before deciding whether to attack, Patton always added a third element to the equation: time. He recognized that time was a resource as critical as men and supplies and, realizing this, he was often prompted to action even when he possessed less than optimum troop strength. His leadership philosophy was always pragmatic, well suited to the imperfect art of war, and, for that matter, to an imperfect world: Use what you have when you have to use it. If you wait for perfection, you will lose opportunity.

85. Plan for Spontaneity

The life of an aircraft pilot depends on his ability to make quick life and death decisions. At the end of the runway before takeoff, the pilot goes through a checklist to make sure the plane is ready to fly. Any mistake in reviewing this checklist and the penalty can be death. Halfway down the runway the pilot must make a second quick decision, namely, is this plane going fast enough to fly or shall the throttle be cut to stay on the ground? The time to make this decision is less than a hundredth of a second. Beyond the halfway point on the runway, the pilot cannot change his decision.

Patton understood the importance of making quick decisions, then never looking back. However, this passage shows that he also understood what goes into a "quick" decision: systematic review and planning. The object is to prepare yourself and others so thoroughly that, when a decision must be made, it can be made immediately and without potentially fatal second-guessing. The decision may consume no more than a split second. The process behind takes as long as prudence demands. Get the facts. Evaluate the facts. And do so *before* a crucial decision is required.

86. Never Give Up Momentum

To hell with taking three days to regroup! We will regroup on the run. Let the women and children consolidate our gains. When we get the enemy on the run, we must keep him on the run. We must run faster than he does! We'll not need food when we are winning! We will eat the enemy!

Momentum is one of the most valuable resources a manager has. It takes a great deal of energy to overcome inertia—to get going—so, once your organization is on the move with a project, it is your job to keep things going. Focus yourself, and focus your resources. Resist the temptation merely to "regroup," to hold your ground, or to "consolidate your gains." Stoke the fires. Maintain the energy.

pate Needs

Timely Thoughts on Supply: Reasonable study and a consultation of the almanac will avoid situations in which, through lack of forethought, heavy clothing, etc., have not been ordered in time. Similarly, a knowledge of the tactical situation will insure that gasoline and ammunition are asked for in time. The Combat Service and not the Supply Service is responsible for failure to get such things.

Know what you need. Anticipate your needs. Ensure that you have what you need *when* you need it. Don't count on somebody else—"the Supply Service"—to know what you need and when you need it. If you don't know what you need, find out before it is too late.

88. The Golden Rule of War

SUCCESS IN WAR DEPENDS UPON THE GOLDEN RULE OF WAR. SPEED—SIMPLICITY—BOLDNESS

—INSCRIBED IN PATTON'S FIELD NOTEBOOK

A plan or course of action driven by speed, simplicity, and boldness is difficult to fault. In most situations, these three qualities are reliable yardsticks against which any idea may be measured.

The best ideas typically have a short shelf life. In business, many circumstances conspire to retard progress. Act as quickly as you can.

Complex plans often look appealing on paper, but tend to fall apart in execution. Keep your plans as simple as is consistent with your objectives.

Cultivate the habit of looking at situations from a fresh perspective. If you find yourself falling thoughtlessly into the well-worn ways of caution, stop, think again, and consider the bolder course.

89. Accent Execution, Not Ideas

Victory in the next war will depend on EXECUTION not PLANS.

—REMARK IN PATTON'S NOTEBOOK, ABOUT 1925

Too many managers devote the bulk of their time to formulating "strategic plans" and the like while ignoring the vital link between plan and action: the *means* of execution. A leader must be part dreamer and part realist. Plans should not be mired in detail, but they must always finally satisfy the demands of detail. Your job is not complete when you have answered *what* is to be done. You must also answer *how* it is to be done.

90. Action Takes Precedence over Plan

Good tactics can save even the worst strategy. Bad tactics will destroy even the best strategy.

Many managers fancy themselves great strategists and draw up sweeping game plans for their organizations. It is a good thing to think big and to stretch yourself, but not at the expense of the everyday necessities required to make your organization run and run efficiently. Never let strategic considerations sweep you away from immediate tactical reality. Plans are nothing if they cannot be executed successfully.

93. Execution Is the Thing

Some day bemused students will try to see how we came to this decision and credit us with profound thought we never had. The thing as I see it is to get a definite, simple plan quickly, and win by execution and careful detailed study of the tactical operation of lesser units. Execution is the thing, that and leadership.

—ON PLANS FOR THE INVASION OF SICILY, 1943

In planning, Patton stressed simplicity and attention to detail in the front lines. For him, plans were nothing more than a broad framework to guide action in the moment as circumstances demanded. He did not believe that battle should be overly rehearsed, but instead he valued spontaneity. Although battle, for him, was never a case of "winging it," he didn't want to be boxed in, either.

Leadership involves establishing a delicate balance between planning and improvisation. What should never be left to chance, however, is the *ability* to execute any plan. Logistics, support, and training should be thoroughly fixed and completely reliable.

92. Always Follow Through

Commanders must remember that the issuance of an order, or the devising of a plan, is only about five percent of the responsibility of command. The other ninety-five percent is to insure, by personal observation, or through the interposing of staff officers, that the order is carried out.

Patton tells us here that leadership is 95 percent follow-through. The trouble is that most senior managers see themselves as strategists and planners, not as monitors or marshals. They must, in fact, be both. Orders and directives are meaningless unless they are carried out and carried out properly and successfully.

93. Aim for the Sweet Spot

There is but one time to do a thing.
That is the first.

—IN HIS WEST POINT NOTEBOOK

Patton was a great believer in formulating alternative plans, yet he also believed that one should never rely on them. In battle, as often in life, second chances are few. "Do not console yourself with the thought, 'I can make a mess of this but next time I will do better,'" West Point Cadet Patton wrote in his notebook. "There is no next time."

6

“The Soldier Is the Army”

On Training, Mentoring, Motivating, Inspiring

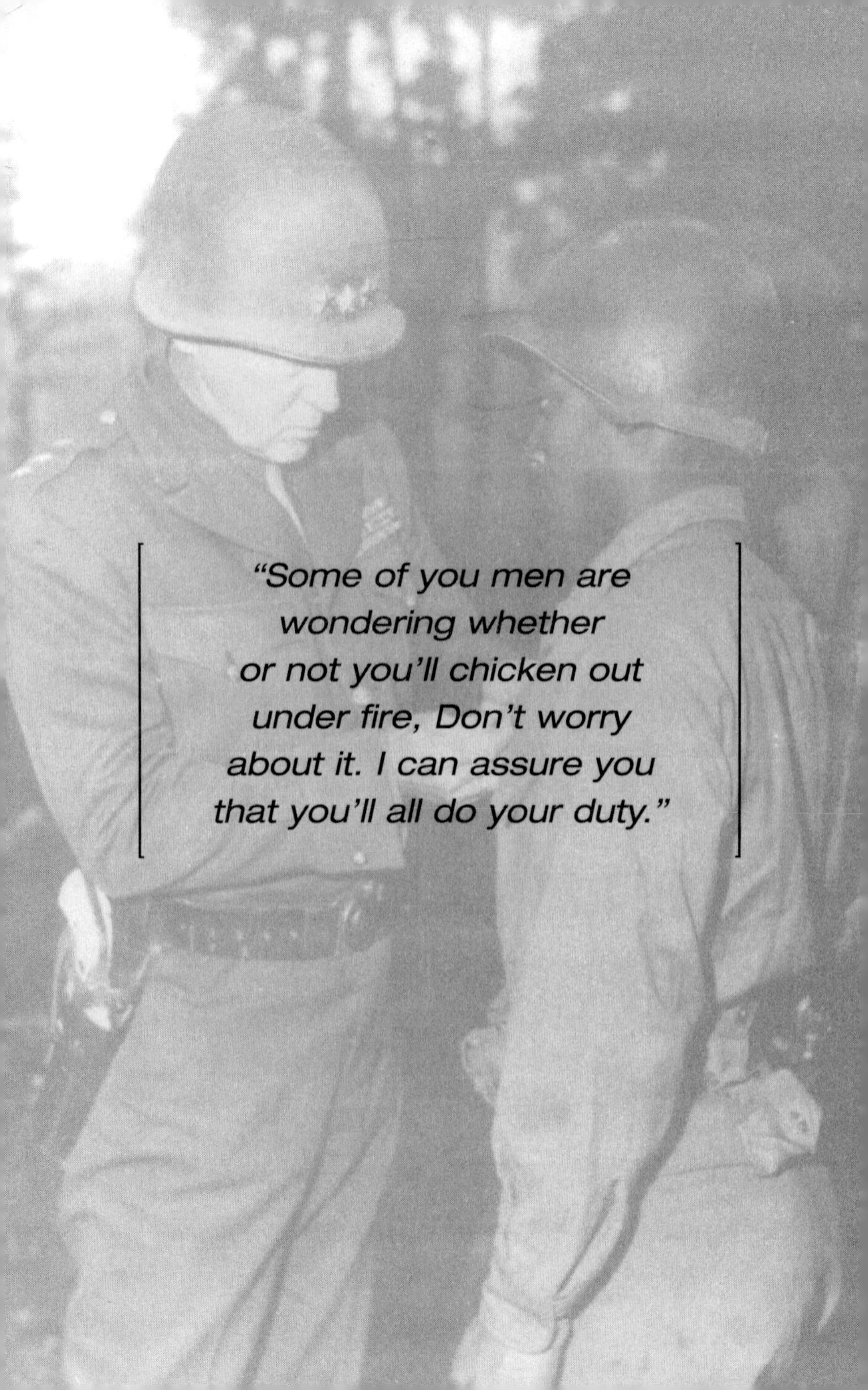

"Some of you men are wondering whether or not you'll chicken out under fire, Don't worry about it. I can assure you that you'll all do your duty."

94. People Are Your Business

The soldier is the army. No army is better than its soldiers.

It is not difficult to translate this observation into civilian terms. No business, firm, or organization is better than the people who run it, who execute the directives of management. This is simple—so simple that it is easy to forget. Too often, managers think of their business in terms of the product it produces.

Think you're in the shoe business?

Think again.

You're in the people business—in the business of recruiting, training, and managing people who happen to make shoes. Shoes are the *by*product of this people business. The *product* is people.

Patton understood that the soldier is the army, and while other—lesser—commanders pored over maps and debated plans of attack, Patton trained, disciplined, and prepared his soldiers. With good soldiers, he knew, the mission—whatever it might be—would be accomplished.

95. The Soldier Really Is the Army

During this operation [the relief of Bastogne and the Battle of the Bulge], the Third Army moved farther and faster and engaged more divisions in less time than any other army in the history of the United States—possibly in the history of the world. The results attained were made possible only by the superlative quality of American officers, American men, and American equipment. No country can stand against such an army.

Between December 19, 1944, and January 16, 1945, Patton moved 17 army divisions an average distance of one hundred miles through ice, snow, and subfreezing weather. The Battle of the Bulge is only one high point in the nine-month history of Patton's Third Army as it marched from the English Channel to the Alps. The army liberated or captured 81,522 square miles of France, 1,010 of Luxembourg, 156 of Belgium, 29,940 of German, 3,485 of Czechoslovakia, and 2,103 square miles of Austria. Some 12,000 cities and towns were liberated or captured.

These results were not produced by heroism alone or even by skill at arms. They were the result of leadership and management of resources—and by Patton's recognition that he was at the head of a superb force, which he had trained.

96. Invest in Human Beings

All this talk about super weapons and push-button warfare is a pile of junk. Man is the only war machine. . . . Always remember that man is the only machine that can win the war. . . . It's nice to have good equipment, . . . but man is the key. Remember the French Revolution? That battle was won with brooms, sticks, and stones—by a bunch of angry women. Get a determined bunch of men and women and they will win the battles no matter what the odds or what kind of equipment they use.

Too many managers are enamored of buildings, machinery, and other equipment. These things are important, but they are nothing without the people to use them. Always put people first. Invest the bulk of your time, attention, and other resources on building a strong team. That is your priority.

97. Everyone Is Expendable

In war every man is expendable. That includes me! Any man who thinks he is indispensable already is not worth his weight in anything. I will a get transfer for such an officer immediately. Every man must be willing to give his life to accomplish the mission, but do not lose your life without making several of the enemy lose theirs. Never die alone. Take several of the enemy with you!

Any man who starts thinking he is indispensable will start staying away from the fighting at the front. He will spend more time in the rear echelons thinking he is too important to risk going where the shells are falling and men are being killed. This man is a coward twice over. He is afraid of himself and of the enemy. In war every man is expendable.

The message here is not that *you* can be replaced. It is a warning against self-importance. A good manager goes where she has to and does what she must. If it means helping out in the front lines—working with a customer, handling a sales call, whatever—don't assume that you are too important to do what's necessary.

98. Train Your Replacement

We can expect that some of us will be killed. We do not want the loss of one man to stop our killing the enemy. Always have a man trained and ready to take over your job in case you are killed. The test of your ability is whether you could be killed and nothing would be lost!

Too many managers are empire builders, who try to arrange things so that they appear indispensable. They don't share information, let alone train their subordinates in any truly meaningful way. They call this selfish and short-sighted approach *self-protection*. In truth, this is bad not only for the organization, it's bad for the individual career.

The effective manager follows Patton's lead here and trains his or her own replacement. An effective manager is a teacher, coach, and mentor. Don't worry, you won't put yourself out of a job—except in an upward direction. Train subordinates to take over, and you make it possible to move up to larger responsibilities.

99. People First

Always remember that it is much better to waste ammunition than lives.

The priorities of a good manager are simple: He or she recognizes that the organization's most valuable assets are its people. "It takes at least eighteen years to produce a soldier, and only a few months to produce ammunition," Patton observed. A trade-off of material resources for human resources is a winning proposition. Never shortsightedly sacrifice people to save a few short-run dollars.

100. A Pound Wise

General Manton S. Eddy called me to state that his allowance of shells for the eighteenth was nine thousand, but I told him to go ahead and shoot twenty thousand, because I could see no reason for hoarding ammunition. You either use it or you don't. I would lose more men by shooting nine thousand rounds a day for three days than I would by shooting twenty thousand in one day—and probably not get as far.

Do not practice foolish economies. Instead, manage resources in a timely fashion. Use them effectively—that is, when they will do the most good.

101. Don't Make Things Harder Than They Have to Be

In a modern infantry division, if every available vehicle—tanks, armored cars, gun carriages, AA guns and trucks—is utilized, no soldier need, or should, walk until he actually enters battle.

Patton's critics were always quick to judge the general as being overly hard on his troops, not only driving them relentlessly to fight, but even demanding that they always wear proper uniforms with full spit and polish. The truth is that Patton *did* demand maximum performance from his troops—and he got what he demanded. He got it because he never made *unnecessary* demands. But he did make demands. For example, in battle (contrary to some legends) he did not insist on keeping uniforms neat and clean, much less on wearing neckties! However, he was adamant that all soldiers wear their helmets at all times. Not only was this part of a "proper combat uniform," it was prudent. Head injuries are common in battle. Wearing a helmet at all times was a lifesaver.

Similarly, Patton believed in using all available *equipment* to preserve the strength and efficiency of *people*. People, he understood, are far more important than equipment. Army regulations permitted a commander to march his infantry troops. But why *march* them when you could *move* them on vehicles that had to be on the move in any case? Nor did Patton restrict transportation of troops to trucks and troop vehicles. *Every* vehicle could carry some troops.

An effective manager uses all resources efficiently. He does not make people work harder for the sake of doing hard work. The necessary and available work is always hard enough as it is. The effective manager uses equipment to serve people. He never puts people in the position of serving the equipment.

102. A Lesson in Loyalty

The other day [Colonel William Darby] was offered the command of a regiment with an increase of one grade in rank, but he refused to take it because he wished to stay with the men he had trained. On the same day, General [Albert C.] Wedemeyer requested to be reduced to a Colonel so that he could take command of a regiment. I consider these two acts outstanding.

—LETTER FROM SICILY, JULY 18, 1943

Loyalty, Patton always insisted, must come not only from the bottom up, but from the top down. The general admired commanders who were intensely loyal to their men and who were willing to forgo promotion to remain hands-on commanders.

103. The Value of Loyalty

I prefer a loyal staff officer to a brilliant one.

You must cultivate a front-line management staff that you can trust. Don't judge the members of your team by raw ability alone. Look at character. And always remember that loyalty flows both ways. If you expect loyalty from those subordinate to you, you must also be prepared to stand by them at every turn.

104. Loyalty Must Be Mutual

There is a great deal of talk about loyalty from the bottom to the top. Loyalty from the top down is even more necessary and much less prevalent.

All managers want and require the loyalty of those they manage. But loyalty is a two-way street. Managers must be loyal to subordinates, and they must ensure that their subordinates are fully aware of their loyalty. Never betray a subordinate's trust. Never use a subordinate as a scapegoat. Never fail to deliver on a promise made to a subordinate. Never exploit those on whom you depend, and never give them even the inkling of a feeling that they are being exploited, cheated, or in any other way treated shabbily.

105. The Two-Way Street

I ordered you to do it, Murnane. So if anything goes wrong, I'll take the blame.

—SPOKEN TO AN OFFICER (MAJ. GEORGE MURNANE) ENTRUSTED WITH A DELICATE TASK

In Normandy, Patton was informed that Eisenhower had assigned a certain general to command a Third Army division, and at once protested (in vain) that he did not want this incompetent so-and-so serving under him. Shortly thereafter Patton's worst fears were realized, when the officer made such a hash of things that Eisenhower directed his relief. "No way," countered Patton to his perplexed friend, who reminded him that he hadn't wanted the general in the first place. "True, but he was one of your spare generals then. Now he's one of my generals. I'll straighten him out myself"; and he did.

—QUOTED IN CARLO D'ESTE, *PATTON: A GENIUS FOR WAR*

Patton's staff officers were often resentful of what they considered the unfair treatment accorded their boss by Eisenhower, but whenever Patton heard such criticism, "he tore the Hell out of us. He really simply would not tolerate such talk on our part. Of course, he'd argue hammer and tongs with Ike in person, but that was a different matter."

—QUOTED IN CARLO D'ESTE,
PATTON: A GENIUS FOR WAR

For Patton, loyalty was always a two-way street. For the manager in any situation, loyalty is not some quaint old code of honor, let alone (as some people insist) a macho rite. It is as necessary as a fair salary and an equal chance at advancement. Maybe it is even more necessary than these things. Loyalty both fuels and lubricates an enterprise.

Contrary to what some managers believe, loyalty is not something simply received from subordinates, like a tax or a tribute. It is always a mutual transaction. You cannot expect loyalty without demonstrating loyalty.

In too many organizations, the prevailing ethic involves a knife in the back. This is, of course, both individually and collectively destructive. Instead, cultivate the sense throughout your organization that, as far as backs are concerned, each member of the group is responsible for watching those of the others. Create loyalty by talking about it and by demonstrating it.

106. Hold Teams Together

Squads should seldom be split.

Patton, a general in command of an entire army—the *largest* military tactical unit, numbering in the hundreds of thousands—also concerned himself with how the *smallest* unit, the squad, consisting of eight to twelve men, should be used. He stressed coordinated teamwork at all times.

Look at this advice: "In river crossings or assault landings, there is a high probability that the boats containing a company or even a platoon will not all land at the same point. Therefore, each boat should be organized on a boat-team basis and contain the means for producing a base of fire and encirclement. These boat teams should practice as such before embarking."

Today, managers are just beginning to catch up with this "small unit" or "team" approach. The effective manager builds discipline and pride in employees, so that they feel a part of the organization on its largest scale. He or she must, however, also foster the development of teams within the larger organization, teams capable of operating in coordination with large units as well as on their own.

107. Build Teams Ruthlessly

Staff officers of inharmonious disposition, irrespective of their ability, must be removed. A staff cannot function properly unless it is a united family.

In a military organization, a commander's staff corresponds to "middle management" in a civilian business. The staff sees to it that the commander's orders are actually, properly, and effectively implemented. The staff is the vital link between a unit's higher headquarters and the various officers in the field. Without a tightly coordinated staff—a harmonious middle-management family—orders will fail to be executed, and the links between headquarters commanders and commanders in the field will be broken.

A manager must ensure that subordinate managers all sing from the same song sheet. This does not mean stamping out individual initiative, but it does mean agreeing on common goals and subordinating to the achievement of these any personal disharmonies or disagreements.

108. The Team Must Be United

A staff cannot function properly unless it is a united family.

A commander's staff is the equivalent of the management team—the people who see to it that decisions and policy are executed. Patton rigorously forged a close team spirit among this inner circle of command. What he called "officers of inharmonious disposition" were removed, even if they were otherwise quite able. Although Patton did not want to surround himself with yes-men, he did want officers who put the mission before personal vanity and personal advancement.

109. Teams Work Miracles

I passed through the last combat team of the 90th Division moving up for battle. These men had been in trucks for a great many hours with the temperature at six degrees below zero, and were thoroughly chilled. On the opposite side of the road was an endless file of ambulances bringing men back—wounded men; yet when the soldiers of the 90th Division saw me, they stood up and cheered. It was the most moving experience of my life, and the knowledge of what the ambulances contained made it still more poignant.

—DURING THE BATTLE OF THE BULGE

Patton understood the value of loyalty. It was loyalty, personally inspired, that helped these men endure subzero temperatures and the sight of the wounded streaming back from the battle to which they were about to be committed.

This is a remarkable passage from Patton's *War As I Knew It.* There is not the slightest tinge of vanity or conceit in this account of a tribute paid to himself. Patton's first and last thoughts, in this passage, are on the price his men pay. And he is profoundly grateful for their willingness to pay it.

110. To Lead Is to Teach

Patton's reputation is built primarily on his success as a commander on the battlefield, but training troops was the foundation of those accomplishments.

—CARLO D'ESTE, *PATTON: A GENIUS FOR WAR*

Whatever else a manager is, he or she must be a mentor, a teacher. In the daily crunch, this aspect of management is all too easily neglected. But consider that the daily crunch is less "crunching" in proportion to the number of trained leaders working with you.

Who will train them?

Why not you?

111. To Teach and to Learn

We can always learn from each other.

—Patton to a junior officer

Patton made it a practice to observe how his men fought and worked, and he listened to them explain how they accomplished their assigned tasks. He believed that the best authority on how to get a job done was the person who *had* to do the job.

Managers should never resist learning even from junior subordinates. By the same token, a good manager is a generous mentor. All worthwhile enterprise involves teaching and learning.

112. Value Experience

We received a number of replacement captains. I initially assigned them to companies under lieutenants until they learned the ropes. While this is not authorized in Regulations, I did it in both this and the First World War, and it works.

Take advantage of experience, even if it means putting a "higher-ranking" employee under the wing of a veteran subordinate for a time. Also note here Patton's attitude toward "The Rules": The best guide is experience, not a rule book. Use what you know works. Discard what you know does not work.

113. Cultivate Experience

War develops a soul in a fighting unit, and while there may not be many of the old men left, it takes very little yeast to leaven a lump of dough.

Two points are key here. The first is the value of experienced hands in an organization. Value your veterans. Put them in mentoring roles. Properly assigned, one or two experienced leaders can readily transform a green crew into an experienced, efficient organization.

The second point is that the identity of an organization may take on a life quite apart from the individuals who happen to make up that organization at any particular point in time. Exploit the identity and pride of your firm. Encourage your employees to identify with the organization.

114. Theory Is Partial Knowledge

Since the necessary limitations of map problems inhibit the student from considering the effects of hunger, emotion, personality, fatigue, leadership, and many other imponderable yet vital factors, he first neglects and then forgets them.

The training of military officers includes a wealth of "map problems," theoretical situations, which may be resolved in the way one resolves a set of algebraic equations or a series of chess moves. The map problem is an important exercise, but it is hardly a substitute for real-world experience with the nontheoretical "imponderables" Patton lists and that the great military thinker Clausewitz called "friction"—all the stubborn realities, large and small, that get between a battle theory and the actual battle.

Value experience above all else. Acquire it actively for yourself. Seek it out in others. In planning a project, resort to the textbooks only *after* you have consulted with people who have actually done and lived through the tasks you are contemplating. Investigate the nature of the "friction" you are likely to encounter. A theoretical understanding of business situations is important, but you must also develop plans to cope with reality.

115. Provide Creative Space

Never tell people how to do things. Tell them what to do and they will surprise you with their ingenuity.

This gives the lie to those who criticize Patton as a micromanager. Patton believed in staying on top of a situation. He believed in gathering as much firsthand information as possible. He believed in monitoring the progress of orders, to ensure that they are carried out fully and successfully. But he also believed in exploiting, encouraging, and rewarding individual initiative. Patton saw leadership as mostly training and motivation. The object of leadership is to create people who know their jobs and who can reliably supply the *how* to your *what.*

116. Demonstrate Confidence

Once, in Sicily, I told a general, who was somewhat reluctant to attack, that I had perfect confidence in him, and that, to show it, I was going home.

A leader needs to have confidence in his subordinates and, equally important, be willing and able to demonstrate his or her confidence in them. Few people want to fail. Most people want to do a good job. Train and prepare the members of your organization, then get out of their way as much as possible. Don't fail to monitor progress, but don't breathe down anyone's neck, either.

117. Let People Do Their Jobs

If you knew your job [in Patton's Third Army] you were allowed to perform it in your own way and were never told how to do a thing, only requested in a quiet gentlemanly way to do it. The rest was up to you. . . . If you didn't, or if you were the cause of any friction . . . you were quickly and quietly gotten rid of, "rolled" as we called it—sent to some other organization.

—COL. BRENTON G. WALLACE, *PATTON AND HIS THIRD ARMY*

Citing Patton's close attention to detail and his insistence on getting out and about to the front lines, some have stamped Patton with the military label "chickenshit." Among soldiers, that term is reserved for an obsession with meaningless detail and make-work assignments. But Patton demonstrated that being detail-oriented and aggressively observant is not the same as being a "chickenshit" commander—or what those of us in business would call a micromanager. The fact is that Patton devoted great energy to choosing a staff who knew their jobs so well that they needed little or no supervision. A continual evaluation of results either confirmed Patton in his choices or prompted him to choose anew.

Too many managers devote the bulk of their energy to "running the business." It is far more effective to focus on finding people who can do the "running" while the manager continually evaluates results and makes personnel-assignment adjustments accordingly. This is not the equivalent of micromanagement on the one hand or trying to let the business run itself on the other. It is putting the focus of management where it can do the most good most of the time.

118. Demonstrate Respect

When a unit has been alerted for inspection, do not fail to inspect it and inspect it thoroughly. Further, do not keep it waiting. When soldiers have gone to the trouble of getting ready to be inspected, they deserve the compliment of a visit. Be sure to tell the unit commander publicly that his unit was good, if such is the case. If it is bad, tell him privately and in no uncertain terms. Be sure to speak to all enlisted men who have decorations, or who have been wounded, and ask how they got the decoration or how they were wounded.

Treat your subordinates with respect and with interest. Both are essential. Employ public praise, but private criticism. Do not criticize a subordinate manager in front of his or her subordinates.

Patton, commanding the 3rd Army, inspects troops of the 2nd Division, in Armagh, Northern Ireland, April 1, 1944.

Patton confers with officers of the 5th Division concerning the process of crossing the Seine, August 26, 1944.

Patton—in France, 1944—poses with a B-17 crew, whose plane had been downed in Germany.

Patton with Lt. Gen. Omar N. Bradley and Brig. Gen. O. P. Weyland, and Patton's dog, Willie, September 29, 1944.

Patton with staff and other officers outside his headquarters in Etain, France, during a visit by Dwight David Eisenhower on September 30, 1944.

American generals gather in Belgium for a visit from King George VI of England.

S.Sgt. Woodrow W. Smith describes the use of a special valve grinder during a Patton visit to the front lines, October 25, 1944.

Patton tours in an armored reconnaissance car near the front lines with Averill Harriman, U.S. ambassador to the Soviet Union, November 27, 1944.

Patton visits an Army-built bridge named after him across the Sauer River, February 20, 1945.

Patton talks to the troops at the Sauer River, February 20, 1945.

George S. Patton, Jr., General, U.S.A., May 1945.

119. Gauge Your Audience

When speaking to a junior about the enemy confronting him, always understate their strength. You do this because the person in contact with the enemy invariably overestimates their strength to himself, so, if you understate it, you probably hit the approximate fact, and also enhance your junior's self-confidence.

The great American poet Emily Dickinson wrote "tell the truth, but tell it slant." This is often sound management advice. On one level, Patton advises slanting the truth in order to avoid intimidating a subordinate—yet, at the same time, this slant involves the senior commander's judgment that the information he is receiving is probably distorted to begin with. Truth, then, may be more fluid than solid.

It takes a wise leader to manage people—and an even wiser one to manage "truth." At the least, you want to avoid discouraging the managers and supervisors who report to you. You don't want to intimidate them. You don't want to induce paralysis in them. Certainly, you should never sugarcoat a critical situation, and you should never deny the existence of obstacles and perils that clearly exist. But it is the natural tendency of most people in charge to overestimate the threat they are facing. To correct this tendency, you may want consciously to understate the threat.

120. Inspire Confidence

During the advance on Messina, along the north road in Sicily, we had made one successful amphibious turning operation and were in the act of executing a second one when, shortly after supper, General Keyes, who was with the 3d Division, telephoned me that General Bradley, commanding the II Corps of which the 3d Division was a unit, and General Truscott, commanding the 3d Division, were both convinced that this second amphibious operation was too dangerous and therefore requested authority to postpone it. I told General Keyes to tell them it would not be postponed and that I would be there at once.

I took General Gay with me, dropping him off at the beach where the amphibious troops were then taking off, with orders to see that they took off. I then went to Headquarters of the 3d Division, which was under limited shell fire, and found General Truscott, a most dashing officer, suffering from such physical fatigue that he was convinced that the operation could not succeed. I directed him to carry it out, stating that if he succeeded he would get the full credit, and that if he failed, I would take the blame. I then called

General Bradley on the telephone and told him the same thing. I stated to both of them that, having complete confidence in them, I was returning to my Headquarters, because if I stayed around I would fail to show confidence. I spent a very restless night, particularly as the enemy was shooting at us, but they failed to get a hit. Shortly after reveille, Colonel Harkins, who was duty officer, called up to say that the attack had been a complete success.

It is a very difficult thing to order two officers in whom you have great confidence to carry out an operation which neither of them thinks is possible.

After reading this brief account from Patton's memoir, *War As I Knew It,* even those otherwise unfamiliar with the general's achievements understand why he was a great leader. Consider the passage carefully.

Patton's guiding principle was to go *forward,* to advance relentlessly against the enemy, and never to relinquish momentum. In accordance with this principle, he refused to postpone an ordered amphibious operation, despite the advice of trusted subordinates. But Patton did not merely bully these subordinates into compliance. Certainly, he had the command authority to do so—to issue an order and demand unquestioning obedience. Yet he understood that this would convey to Bradley and Truscott a lack of confidence in them, and if these commanders suspected that Patton did not trust them, they would lose confidence in themselves, they would resent Patton, and they would never again be able to give him their full loyalty. With great brilliance of leadership, Patton exacted compliance, but also preserved the delicate bond between him and his subordinates. First, he removed as much of the risk from their shoulders as possible, promising them the credit for success and pledging to take upon himself the burden of failure. Second, he had the great courage to return to headquarters and let his two subordinates do the job he had assigned to them.

This passage contains perhaps the hardest lessons a leader has to learn. There is a tissue-thin line separating self-confidence from blind foolishness, and it is also a matter of great artfulness and moral courage to issue orders and directives without undermining the confidence of subordinates and without jeopardizing a close working relationship with them.

121. The Use of Discipline

There has been, and is now, a great deal of talk about discipline; but few people, in or out of the Army, know what it is or why it is necessary.

Anyone who has seen the movie *Patton* remembers how the general shook things up when he took command of the *losing* American army in North Africa. Among other measures, he ordered these combat soldiers to wear full and proper uniforms, including neckties. Doubtless many who have seen the film find it hard to believe that a commanding general in a war zone would worry about whether or not his soldiers sported neckties.

But Patton did indeed concern himself with neckties, because he understood that a great deal more was at stake than a military fashion statement. Patton's original "necktie order" was issued not in North Africa, but months earlier, in the United States, at the Desert Training Center near Indio, California.

"We have reached the stage in our desert training," he told a staff meeting, "where there is no excuse for any soldier not to be clean and in proper uniform. . . . Army regulations will be enforced. No man, officer or enlisted man, leaves this post without being in proper uniform. And that uniform better be clean! He must be wearing the insignia of I Armored Corps on his arm below his left shoulder. Any man out of uniform or with long hair and dirt stays on the post. No man can have any pride if he looks as if he has to go to the bathroom or has just been there!"

At first, there was no particular mention of neckties. Then Patton found out that soldiers going out on leave were removing their neckties and taking off their blouses (the term for the jacket part of the uniform) after they got past the guards at the main gate. In response, Patton added the necktie provision. Consider it carefully before writing Patton off as nothing more than a hard case who liked to throw his weight around.

The order stated that any officer or noncommissioned officer who saw a soldier out of uniform *anywhere* was to stop the soldier and get his name and company. If any company commander had two of his men reported, he would have to write a detailed letter explaining why the men were out of uniform. If *three* soldiers from the same company were discovered out of uniform, the company commander would be ordered to resign or face court martial.

Thus Patton put the real pressure on commanders, not on the men. Using the uniform issue, he compelled his commanders to exercise "remote control" over their men. Discipline was thus enforced off-post as well as on.

But how did the men feel about this?

Perhaps surprisingly, they did not grumble. Instead, they started to take great pride in their spit-and-polish appearance, which set them apart from soldiers in other military organizations. They were *"Patton's men."* They looked sharper than other soldiers. They even saluted sharper. (In the army of World War II, to "give a George Patton" meant to give a particularly snappy hand salute.) Soon, it was naturally assumed that they were better soldiers. Certainly, they *felt* as if they were the best.

"All human beings," Patton wrote, "have an innate resistance to obedience. Discipline removes this resistance, and, by constant repetition, makes obedience habitual and subconscious. Where would an undisciplined football team get?

The players react subconsciously to the signals. They must, because the split second required for thought would give the enemy the jump." Patton continued:

> *Battle is much more exigent than football. No sane man is unafraid in battle, but discipline produces in him a form of vicarious courage which, with his manhood, makes for victory. Self-respect grows directly from discipline. The Army saying, "Who ever saw a dirty soldier with a medal?" is largely true.*

Obedience? Is that really what the nonmilitary manager wants? Probably not. But compliance, cooperation, and coordination are always important, as is a commitment to doing the job well. These qualities come with discipline and pride, and the manager cannot afford to assume that these traits are inborn in all employees. Enforce high standards of appearance and conformity to *worthwhile* rules—not for the sake of mere appearance or conformity, but to instill discipline and pride.

122. The Effect of Discipline

On 6 March 1943 Patton was assigned as Commanding General II Corps and he hit them like "Moses descending from Mount Ararat." But instead of the Ten Commandments he brought his own personal text of severe, unrelenting discipline. He motored around all the units, down to battalion level, escorted by siren-screeching scout cars and half-tracks, all bristling with weapons and covered in the largest stars his aides could produce. No unit was spared from his blistering speeches, and such regulations as wearing ties, leggings, helmets, and sidearms, and shaving every day were rigorously enforced. "At this point [according to one Patton biographer, Alden Hatch] Patton was probably the most unpopular commander in American history. But something happened to II Corps. It became, in spite of itself, a Patton army—the first one—tough and bitter and proud; capable of doing the impossible, and then going out the next day and doing it again."

—George Forty,
The Armies of George S. Patton

Patton assumed command of II Corps in North Africa after it had suffered a stunning defeat in the U.S. Army's first contest with the Germans, at the Kasserine Pass. Whether they realize it or not, all managers establish a "contract" with the people they lead. From day one, Patton forged a contract that was as uncompromising as it was dramatic. He created discipline from the ground up, paying close attention to the details that compelled the men of his command to behave in every respect like soldiers. At the same time, he made certain that the men from whom he demanded so much were always fairly treated, justifiably praised, and adequately supplied with everything they needed to carry out his orders.

123. Discipline: A Definition

There is only one kind of discipline.
Perfect discipline.

Be uncompromising in areas that permit no compromise, such as issues of quality, concentration, and productivity. In the truly important aspects of your enterprise, do not hesitate to ask for a great deal from yourself and from those you supervise. You and the others will discover new levels of performance. But you have to demand it—and expect it.

124. Personalize Leadership

I'm proud to be here to fight beside you. Now let's cut the guts out of those Krauts and get the hell on to Berlin. And when we get to Berlin, I am going to personally shoot that paper-hanging son of a bitch just as I would a snake.

—Address to his troops, July 6, 1944

Mediocre managers hide behind such phrases as "management believes" or "pursuant to company policy." Genuine leaders, however, personalize leadership. Patton repeatedly emphasized the officer's role as fighting side by side with his men, sharing their hardships and their risks. He also reduced war to personal terms—as in this quotation—that he felt his men could better identify with.

125. The Role of Personal Inspiration

It's the cold glitter of the attacker's eye, not the point of the questing bayonet, that breaks the line. It's the fierce determination of the driver to close with the enemy, not the mechanical perfection of the tank, that conquers the trench. It's the cataclysmic ecstacy of conflict in the flier, not the perfection of his machine gun, which drops the enemy in flaming ruin. Yet volumes are devoted to armaments; and only pages to inspiration.

Patton wrote this in 1926, in a brief statement he called "The Secret of Victory." Most managers have no trouble believing in the value of good computers, reliable phone lines, top-of-the-line fax machines, and every other piece of hardware associated with their business or industry. But few managers believe in the power of inspiration. It's corny, they say. No one really believes it anymore.

The truth is that most of us are afraid to admit the power of inspiration. We're afraid to believe that, ultimately, our success doesn't depend on having better computers or milling machines than our competitors, but on being motivated by greater inspiration than they are. The idea of careers and millions of dollars in capital and profits riding on *emotions* is scary.

But it's also a fact.

In the "Secret of Victory," Patton wrote of "that vitalizing spark, intangible, yet as evident as lightning—The Warrior Soul." On it, the product of inspiration, more than on tanks, planes, and guns, victory depends. Patton's greatness as a military leader—and his effectiveness as a manager of people—was his courageous willingness to recognize that his career, his life, the lives of his men, the welfare of his nation, *everything,* ultimately depended on his ability to be inspired by and to inspire others.

Never neglect technology, Patton would advise. "Every tank and every truck is as different as every man," Patton told his officers at the Desert Training Center in Indio, California. "Make sure every driver knows his tank or truck. He must know exactly how many gallons of gas and oil is needed for a mile and for an hour—and at different speeds and conditions. Check the tank every time it is refueled. If it is using too much of anything, send it to heavy maintenance. We must *know* our equipment." Never neglect technology, but never forget that victory depends on maintenance of the spirit as much as it does on the maintenance of machines.

126. Group Personality

It is an unfortunate fact that few commanders, and no politicians, realize the individuality of units and the necessity of playing on human emotion. Speaking of this reminds me that [General Willard S.] Paul once told me, with perfect sincerity, that the greatest moment of his life had been at the Battle of the Bulge when I put my arm around him and said, "How is my little fighting son of a bitch today?" He said that this remark inspired not only him, but every man in the division, and it is highly probable that it did.

Effective leaders never neglect and always cultivate the human touch. Make contact with your subordinates. Communicate with them on a caring, comradely, good-natured level. Demonstrate not only your confidence and pride in them, but your affection as well. If you find it difficult to express emotion in this way, *try* nevertheless. If you believe that human contact is incompatible with "professionalism," rethink your definition of *professionalism.*

127. Inside Inspiration

[Patton] really inspired everybody with the idea that when you have gone just as far as you can go, you can still go a little bit further. . . . You might not have loved him, but you respected him and admired him and you wanted to put out for him. . . . Every unit in the division developed a very fierce and intense pride in its accomplishments.

—MAJ. ISAAC D. WHITE

A true leader gets inside those he leads. He does not impose commands from the outside, but inspires people to draw on their own deepest inner reserves. Effective leadership is inspiration. An effective leader is a catalyst who does not *force* change but *enables* change in others.

128. Inspiration à la Patton

I am the best damn ass-kicker
in the whole U.S. Army!

Well, substitute a milder noun—perhaps "motivator"—and you have a goal to which any manager might aspire. Keep your focus on people, not products, not sales, not whatever it is your organization produces. In order to do whatever it does and create whatever it creates, your organization must first motivate people and keep them motivated. That is your number-one job as a manager.

129. Taking Care of Business

As a whole, the men were poor,
the officers worse; no drive. It is very sad.
I saw one lieutenant let his men hesitate
to jump into the water. I gave him hell.

—PATTON DIARY ENTRY ON THE LANDING
OF HIS WESTERN TASK FORCE IN NORTH AFRICA

Patton watched and drew conclusions. He had an uncanny ability to go straight to the heart of a problem and then intervene personally to correct it. He attended immediately to any problems he saw.

130. Sort of a Kick

On the twenty-eighth of July, 1944, General Bradley informed me that the Third Army would become operational at noon on August 1, but that in the interim I was to take over control of the VIII and XV Corps—this without becoming officially connected with the operations. On the afternoon of the twenty-ninth, south of Coutances, I found an armored division halted on the road while the Headquarters was having a map study as to the possibility of crossing the Sienne River with a view to advancing along the coast road toward Granville. Taking a glance at the map, I saw that the river was within a few miles, so went down and reconnoitered it. I found it was only about two feet deep and, so far as I could tell, defended by one machine gun which missed me by a good deal. Fortified with this information, I went back to the Commanding General and asked him why he didn't get across the river. He said be didn't know whether the tide was in or out, and that he understood the river was strongly defended. I told him in very strong language what I had just done and to get a move on himself, which he did. From that time on, this division was one of the boldest in the Third Army, but since this was its initiation to battle, it needed just that sort of a kick to get it started.

A big part of managing is knowing when to get up out of your chair and *go forward* to the front lines. Patton had an instinct for when to take matters into his own hands. Why study a map and rely on secondhand information when you could investigate the situation for yourself? While the commander of the stalled armored division scratched his head over a map, Patton obtained the facts, delivered the facts, and ordered action on the facts. Unfortunately, few managers have the instinct and consistent energy for such action. Most are like the map-reading commanding general. Even more unfortunate, however, is the fact that, of the few managers who might take a see-for-yourself approach similar to Patton's, even fewer would conclude the incident as generously as Patton does. A lesser manager than Patton would have simply concluded this account with self-congratulatory grumbling to the effect of "If you want something done, do it yourself," but Patton believed that his action was nothing more than a catalyst. Instead of denigrating the unit in question or its commander, Patton observed that he administered a "sort of kick to get it started" and that it went on to become one of the "boldest" units in the Third Army. You have gained nothing if your leadership action achieves some particular objective (such as crossing a river) but tears down a subordinate in the process. Leadership action must achieve immediate objectives even as it builds independence and initiative in subordinates.

Later in July 1944, Patton had a conference with General Troy H. Middleton, commander of the Third Army's VIII Corps.

> *I told General Middleton . . . that I was taking over in the morning. He said he was glad I had arrived because he had obtained his objective, which was the Selune River. I asked him if he was across and he said, "No." I told him that throughout history, many campaigns had been lost by stopping on the wrong side of a river, and directed him to go across at once. He said that the bridge below Avranches was out. While we were discussing ways and means of getting across, a telephone message came in that the bridge, while*

> *damaged, was usable—further, that the 4th Armored Division had captured a dam to the east of Avranches, across which troops could move. I directed that the VIII Corps start across that night, which it did. This is no criticism of General Middleton, who is an outstanding soldier, but it shows that a little extra push at a critical moment is sometimes useful. Had we failed to secure a bridgehead that night, our whole operation would have been jeopardized.*

"A little extra push" is often the most important tool in a manager's leadership toolbox.

131. Personal Best

Patton's wife, Beatrice, found her husband kneeling in prayer before a polo match. "Afterward she asked what he'd been praying for. 'For help in the polo game,' he replied. 'Were you praying for a win?' she inquired. 'Hell no,' he said. 'I was praying to do my best.'"

—QUOTED IN CARLO D'ESTE, *PATTON: GENIUS FOR WAR*

Shakespeare said it: "The fault . . . lies not in our stars, but in ourselves." Just as Patton was willing to shoulder the responsibility for the failure of an enterprise, so he also understood that the seeds of success lay within himself. For strength, he looked within—not to outside circumstance. Intensely competitive, he always saw his ultimate competitor as himself.

132. Corporate Best

We are the best and don't ever forget it! Don't let anybody forget that we are the best!

A good leader is never bashful about instilling pride in the organization. Set the bar high—higher even than you think reality warrants—and the people in your organization will raise themselves to meet it. Persuade your subordinates, colleagues, and bosses that "we are the best," and the *best* of those people will rise to meet your appraisal.

133. Neutralizing Fear

There is nothing to combat! It is just like the fear of getting married. When you have dated every girl in the neighborhood, you have enough sense to get married or stay single. You have the facts! When you get the best training for combat and have the best equipment, you are ready to kill the enemy. You can forget your fears and get the job done. There will be a shot that might fall close now and then, but nothing to worry about. Combat is like a marriage. A stray shot now and then is like a spat with your wife—could make the marriage better. The more combat time we can get the better we will be. Combat will make all of us better soldiers.

—Patton lecture remarks reported by Lt. Porter B. Williamson

Fear is mostly fear of the unknown. You can manage fear in yourself and in those you lead by doing as much as possible to eliminate the unknown. As Patton would say, *get the facts,* and, as he points out here, prepare yourself with the best equipment and the best training. Then step boldly into the fray. Difficult and demanding situations make us stronger and better at what we do. Embrace difficulty as an opportunity for growth.

134. Productive Rivalry

I told each Corps Commander that I expected him to get there first, so as to produce a proper feeling of rivalry.

—PATTON ON THE THIRD ARMY'S RACE TO THE RHINE

It is folly to create destructive, backstabbing rivalries among subordinate managers, but a skillful leader is not above nurturing a good-natured, yet earnest rivalry, especially when it is directed toward a specific goal.

135. Avoid Negativity

Do not place military cemeteries where they can be seen by replacements marching to the front. This has a very bad effect on morale, even if it adds to the pride of the Graves Registration Service.

The advice is obvious enough to military planners. For civilian managers, the lesson is also obvious: Don't go out of your way to introduce negativity into the workplace. Don't greet new employees with horror stories about how hard it is to make a buck in the business. Don't welcome the new guy with tales about how his predecessor had failed. Without abandoning reality, usher in new employees with as much *positive* truth as possible.

136. Cultivate a Feel for Appropriate Celebration and Ceremony

I flew to Mainz [to ceremonially open a military] railway bridge over the Rhine . . . . I was asked to cut the red tape, in lieu of a red ribbon, to open the bridge, and was handed a pair of scissors. However, my romantic instinct prompted me to ask for a bayonet with which I cut the tape.

No one had a keener awareness than Patton of the importance of ceremony to aid morale and to create solidarity of purpose among the troops. Patton always carried off ceremonial occasions with flair and originality.

Too few managers take time for ceremonies, for occasions on which group identity is defined and affirmed. And when ceremonies *are* observed, too often they are carried out in a dull, hollow, perfunctory fashion. Whatever else a manager is in a practical, roll-up-your-sleeves sense, he or she is also a symbol of leadership. Take advantage of ceremonial occasions as a stage on which to exhibit yourself as a leader. If necessary, *create* appropriate occasions.

137. Praise Must Be Timely and Public

Gen. Patton [installed a radio system on base, which he] used to commend special efforts by the troops. He would announce, "Found a damn good soldier today!" He would continue, giving the name of the man and the organization.

—Lt. Porter B. Williamson,
recalling a Patton leadership technique

Effective leaders identify and publicly credit exceptional achievement. This is crucial to reinforcing the level of productivity and quality you want. It celebrates achievement and lifts morale, and it provides incentive to further achievement. It is an indispensable management technique.

138. Praise Must Be Personal and Sincere

In October, [Gen. George C.] Marshall visited Third Army where he decorated a soldier with the Silver Star for breaking up a German counterattack by destroying three Tiger tanks with a bazooka. After Marshall had finished, Patton asked if he might be permitted to make a presentation of his own. "On the spot Georgie composed an inspiring citation of his own and presented the soldier with the DSC [Distinguished Service Cross] which his aide quickly supplied. Can you wonder that the men of the Third Army were willing to follow Georgie to the end of the world?"

—Gen. William H. Hobson,
quoted in Carlo D'Este, *Patton: A Genius for War*

No management tool is more powerful than sincere personal praise delivered publicly and in a timely manner. Patton was a great believer in medals and awards, provided that they were issued publicly and as soon as possible after the event in question. Prompt positive reinforcement in the form of commemoration and celebration is essential to the morale of any organization. Few managers devote sufficient attention to this.

139. Praise Must Be Precise and Detailed

TO BE READ TO TROOPS

Soldiers of the Seventh Army and
XII Air Support Command:

Landed and supported by the navy and air force, you have, during twenty-one days of ceaseless battle and unremitting toil, killed and captured more than 87,000 enemy soldiers, you have captured or destroyed 361 cannon, 172 tanks, 928 trucks, and 190 airplanes—you are magnificent soldiers! General Eisenhower, the Commander-in-Chief, and General Alexander, the Army Group Commander, have both expressed pride and satisfaction in your efforts.

Now in conjunction with the British Eighth Army you are closing in for the kill. Your relentless offensive will continue to be irresistible.
The end is certain and is very near.
Messina is our next stop!

—General Order Number 10, after taking Palermo, Sicily

A good leader is generous with praise, and, equally important, he or she makes the praise genuine. It is always a good idea to review and announce your organization's accomplishments. Do this by telling the members of the organization just what they have accomplished. Back up this information with facts; real live numbers are always most effective.

By definition, congratulations concern the past—what has just been accomplished. However, congratulatory messages should always end by looking to the future. Note the closing paragraph of Patton's message. It gives a progress report ("you are closing in") *and* a prediction of "irresistible" success.

140. Praise Must Look Forward as Well as Back

I desire to express to all ranks my sincere appreciation of your magnificent performance. Your untiring effort on training has made you a great division. When you meet the enemy, the same spirit of devotion will make you feared and famous. I shall be very proud of you.

—Message to the 2nd Armored Division, after Patton was promoted to higher command

Take every opportunity presented to convey *convincing* praise. The function of praise is to encourage continued superior performance while setting the bar a little bit higher. Always end messages of congratulation or praise with a look toward the future.

141. Be Generous with Credit

During the course of this war I have received promotion and decorations far above and beyond my individual merit. You have won them: I as your representative wear them. The one honor which is mine and mine alone is that of having commanded such an incomparable group of Americans, the record of whose fortitude, audacity and valor will endure as long as history lasts.

—FROM PATTON'S GENERAL ORDER FOR V-E DAY

Generosity is a quality of leadership too often overlooked. Patton, whom many criticized as being hungry for glory, was always eager to credit his men for all that he had accomplished. Include everyone in every accomplishment.

142. A Masterpiece of Praise

A General Officer who will invariably assume the responsibility for failure, whether he deserves it or not, and invariably give the credit for success to others, whether they deserve it or not, will achieve outstanding success. In any case, letters of commendation and General Orders presenting to the command the glory and magnitude of their achievements have a great influence on morale.

Critics and a hostile press missed no opportunity to accuse Patton of glory grabbing, but anyone who studies the historical record will find that Patton continually issued commendations and bestowed praise on the members of his command. On March 23, 1945, Patton published General Order Number 70, congratulating his army on what it had accomplished. It is vintage Patton:

> *To the Officers and Men of the Third Army*
>
> *and*
>
> *To Our Comrades of the XIX Tactical Air Command*
>
> *In the period from January 29 to March 22, 1945, you have wrested 6,484 square miles of territory from the enemy. You have taken 3,072 cities, towns, and villages, including among the former: Trier, Koblenz, Bingen, Worms, Mainz, Kaiserslautern, and Ludwigshafen.*
>
> *You have captured 140,112 enemy soldiers, and have killed or wounded an additional 99,000, thereby eliminating practically all of the German 7th and 1st Armies. History records no greater achievement in so limited a time.*

This great campaign was only made possible by your disciplined valor, unswerving devotion to duty, coupled with the unparalleled audacity and speed of your advance on the ground; while from the air, the peerless fighter-bombers kept up a relentless round-the-clock attack upon the disorganized enemy.

The world rings with your praises; better still, General Marshall, General Eisenhower, and General Bradley have all personally commended you. The highest honor I have ever attained is that of having my name coupled with yours in these great events.

Please accept my heartfelt admiration and thanks for what you have done, and remember that your assault crossing over the Rhine at 2200 hours last night assures you of even greater glory to come.

Take a close look at this remarkable document. It is a model of how to praise subordinates. Begin by inventorying pronouns. The word *you* is used over and over again, while the pronoun *I* appears only once—and that in a sentence declaring that the highest honor Patton has ever attained is "that of having my name linked with yours in these great events." The effective manager puts the focus on the people managed, not on him- or herself. Of equal importance, note the sparing use of adjectives and the generous use of facts. Patton summarizes with precise, concrete figures and names just what the Third Army has accomplished: 6,484 square miles of territory taken, 140,112 prisoners captured, and so on. The problem with most praise is that it is empty, ringing hollow with vague adjectives. The most effective, persuasive praise is a precise tally of accomplishments, names, dates, figures, and effects.

Finally, look at the last paragraph. Congratulations should never remain focused on past events. Patton gives full credit to his troops for what they have *done,* then ends by using their accomplishments to predict even greater glory in the immediate future. Praise, after all, is motivation, and motivation is by definition directed to the future.

7

"Letters of Instruction"

On Communication and Coordination

“Plans must be
simple and flexible.”

143. Define Goals and Expectations

Letters of Instruction

On March 6, 1944, General Patton issued Letter of Instruction Number 1 to his corps, division, and separate unit commanders to "orient you, officers of the higher echelons, in the principles of command, combat procedure, and administration which obtain in this Army." The Letter is filled with sound management advice.

Under the headings "II. Command, a. Leadership," Patton wrote:

> *(1) Full Duty*
>
> *Each, in his appropriate sphere, will lead in person. Any commander who fails to obtain his objective, and who is not dead or severely wounded, has not done his full duty.*
>
> *(2) Visits to Front*
>
> *The Commanding General or his Chief of Staff (never both at once) and one member of each of the General Staff sections, the Signal, Medical, Ordnance, Engineer, and Quartermaster sections, should visit the front daily. . . .*
>
> *The function of these . . . officers is to observe, not to meddle. In addition to their own specialty, they must observe and report anything of military importance. Remember that praise is more valuable than blame. Remember, too, that your primary mission as a leader is to see with your own eyes and be seen by your troops while engaged in personal reconnaissance.*

Under the heading "II. Command, b. Execution," Patton observed that "In carrying out a mission, the promulgation of the order represents not over ten percent of your responsibility. The remaining ninety percent consists in assuring by means of personal supervision on the ground, by yourself and your staff, proper and vigorous execution." Yet Patton also prescribed strict observance of rest periods:

> *Staff personnel, commissioned and enlisted, who do not rest, do not last. All sections must run a daily roster and enforce compliance. The intensity of Staff operations during battle is periodic. At the Army and Corps levels the busiest times are the periods from one to three hours after daylight, and from three to five hours after dark. In the lower echelons and in the administrative and supply Staffs, the time of the periods is different, but just as definite. When the need arises, everyone must work all the time, but these emergencies are not frequent: unfatigued men last longer and work harder at high pressure.*

Under "III. Combat Procedure, a. Maps": "We are too prone to believe that we acquire merit solely through the study of maps in the safe seclusion of a Command Post. This is an error." Patton demanded that his senior officers survey the situation from the front, not from the safety of a map room.

Under "b. Plans," Patton observed that "Plans must be simple and flexible. Actually, they only form a datum plane from which you build as necessity directs or opportunity offers. They should be made by the people who are going to execute them." He continued, under the heading of "Reconnaissance": "You can never have too much reconnaissance. Use every means available before, during, and after battle. Reports must be facts, not opinions; negative as well as positive. . . . Information is like eggs: the fresher the better."

Patton cautioned his commanders to keep their orders short, "get them out in time; issue them personally by voice when you can" and to "use every means before and after combats to tell the troops what they are going to do and what they have done."

Under "IV. Administration, a. Supply," Patton wrote: "The onus of supply rests equally on the giver and the taker. Forward units must anticipate needs and ask for supplies in time. They must stand ready to use all their means to help move supplies." But Patton also directed that the supply service act proactively, "by reconnaissance, they will anticipate demands and start the supplies up before they are called for."

Patton was a great believer in military decorations, explaining in his Letter of Instruction that they "are for the purpose of raising the fighting value of troops; therefore they must be awarded promptly. Have a definite officer on your staff educated in writing citations and see that they get through."

As for discipline, "There is only one kind of discipline—PERFECT DISCIPLINE. If you do not enforce and maintain discipline, you are potential murderers. You must set the example." And the subject of courage is treated in a single sentence (borrowed from General Thomas "Stonewall" Jackson): "DO NOT TAKE COUNSEL OF YOUR FEARS."

On April 3, Patton issued a "Confidential" Letter of Instruction Number 2. Let's take a close look at some of it:

> *Discipline is based on pride in the profession of arms, on meticulous attention to details, and on mutual respect and confidence. Discipline must be a habit so ingrained that it is stronger than the excitement of battle or the fear of death.*

How many managers would define "discipline" in so positive a way—in terms of pride, attention to detail, respect, and confidence? Too few, unfortunately. For most of us, discipline is mostly a matter of negatives: the ability to avoid temptation, to avoid laziness, to put off doing what we *really* want to do. Patton, however, understood that an effective leader frames discipline in positive, desirable terms and embraces it not as something imposed from the outside, but as a trait—a habit—that comes from a deep internal need to excel.

> *The history of our invariably victorious armies demonstrates that we are the best soldiers in the world. This should make your men proud. This should make you proud. This should imbue your units with unconquerable self-confidence and pride in demonstrated ability.*

Many managers become self-consciously tongue-tied at the thought of giving a "pep talk" or saying something to build pride in their organization. Patton, in contrast, never felt himself at such a loss. It is important for a leader to demonstrate pride in his organization and to persuade the members of that organization to share his pride. Look at the carefully chosen words of the first sentence of the passage quoted above. The words "history," "invariably," and "demonstrates" are powerful persuaders that transform Patton's assessment of his soldiers as the "best soldiers in the world" from opinion to fact.

> *Officers must assert themselves by example and by voice. They must be pre-eminent in courage, deportment, and dress.*

Leaders must lead by example and must constantly display the qualities and values held in esteem by the organization.

> *Combat experience has proven ceremonies such as formal guard mounts, formal and regular and supervised reveille formations, are a great help, and, in some cases, essential, to prepare men and officers for battle, to give them that perfect discipline, that smartness of appearance, that alertness without which battles cannot be won.*

Today's managers typically minimize ceremonial occasions, such as awards presentations, commemorations, facilities dedications, and so on. Patton understood the importance of ceremonial occasions to enforce discipline and to create feelings of pride and group solidarity.

There are significant similarities between business and warfare. In Patton's approach to battle tactics, the civilian manager can find much of value:

> *Hit hard soon . . . develop your maximum force at once before the enemy can develop his.*

Take decisive action with a maximum effort. Halfway measures tip your hand to the competition.

> *Never yield ground. It is cheaper to hold what you have than to retake what you have lost.*

When you invest time, effort, and other resources in acquiring something—technology, a market share, a valued employee, whatever—continue to invest in holding on to that resource. The same may be said about customers and clients. Remember that your *best* customers and clients are those you currently have. It is cheaper to hold on to them than it is to acquire new ones.

> *Take plenty of time to set up an attack. It takes at least two hours to prepare an infantry battalion to execute a properly coordinated attack. Shoving them in too soon produces useless losses.*

Never confuse speed with haste. Devote time to preparations directly related to an operation or project. Committing resources to a poorly prepared project is a waste of those resources.

> *Sharpen axes, pickaxes, and shovels now, and keep them sharp.*

Pay attention to the dozens of unglamorous support items that are necessary to the success of a project, and be certain that they are in place and ready to go before the endeavor is launched. Don't put off the important routine jobs.

> *Officers and men must know their equipment. They must train with the equipment they intend to use in battle. Equipment must be in the best operational condition when taken to the Theater of Operations.*

A manager must ensure that her subordinates know their jobs, know the essential procedures, and know how to use essential equipment. Don't leave any of these basics to chance.

> *There is a universal failure to repeat oral orders back. This failure is certain to result in grave error.*

Many—perhaps most—failures of management are really failures of communication. Establish procedures to ensure error-free communication and to make certain that your directives are heard and understood.

> *Messages and orders must use concise military verbiage.*

Keep directives as short as is compatible with their being fully understood. Don't waste words. This uses up time, and it creates confusion. If your business or organization has certain well-defined and universally understood terms, be certain to use them.

> *There is a tendency for the chain of command to overload junior officers by excessive requirements in the way of training and reports. You will alleviate this burden by eliminating nonessential demands.*

Managers should relentlessly and repeatedly review procedures and requirements to weed out anything that is nonessential or smacks of "make-work." Streamline wherever possible, always stopping short of compromising quality or systems of genuinely prudent checks and balances.

Junior officers of reconnaissance units must be very inquisitive. Their reports must be accurate and factual. Negative information is as important as positive information. . . . All members of a reconnaissance unit should know what they are trying to do. The results of all reconnaissance obtained in front of one division must be transmitted to adjacent units.

In most business situations, information is by far the most valuable commodity. Ask question, and encourage your subordinates at every level to ask questions. Share the information in a timely manner with all members of your organization who will benefit from access to the information.

Officers are responsible, not only for the conduct of their men in battle, but also for their health and contentment when not fighting. An officer must be the last man to take shelter from fire, and the first to move forward. Similarly, he must be the last man to look after his own comfort at the close of a march. He must see that his men are cared for. The officer must constantly interest himself in the rations of the men. He should know his men so well that any sign of sickness or nervous strain will be apparent to him, and he can take such action as may be necessary.

Your human resources must not merely be "managed," but cared for and, in a very real sense, nurtured. Take time to talk to the people in your organization. Learn about what interests and concerns them. A clearly caring attitude will yield high performance dividends.

144. Put the Mission in a Fresh Light

When we land we will meet German and Italian soldiers whom it is our honor and privilege to attack and destroy. . . . The glory of American arms, the honor of our country, the future of the world rests in your individual hands.

—MESSAGE TO THE TROOPS PRIOR TO THE LANDING IN SICILY, JULY 1943.

Define your mission in a way that puts it in a perspective that may not be immediately available or apparent to the people you manage. The phrase "honor and privilege" puts the grim task ahead into a startlingly effective light, and note how Patton stresses *individual* responsibility in an immense and profound undertaking. One of his great talents as a leader was the ability to make the war—this great, confusing, terrifying, violent, yet often abstract enterprise—immediately and dramatically relevant to each and every member of his command, from general to private.

145. Cut to the Chase

Remember, wars are won by killing people. The more we kill, the quicker we'll get out of this war. Wars are not won by defending land. Let the enemy have any land he wants as long as we can get him into a position where we can kill him.

Like such great American generals as Ulysses S. Grant and William Tecumseh Sherman, George S. Patton had a faculty for cutting through the pomp and circumstance and getting to the heart of war. War is about killing. The rest is byproduct and side effect.

All successful leaders know, above all, what they are doing. They know what the goal or goals are. They focus all activity on achieving those goals and do not allow themselves—or the people they lead—to get distracted by byproducts and side effects.

146. Be Sure the Goals You Define Are Worth Winning

So many battles are fought in war and in civilian life, and nothing is gained by the victory. Every battle we fight will result in a gain for us or we will not fight. . . . There is no great gain in merely being right. To be right about some unimportant subject is not important.

Choose your battles. Having chosen a battle, win it. But, first, choose. An aggressive spirit of leadership is valuable, but pointless aggression is worse than useless. It is destructive of resources, of people, and of morale.

147. Shun Motives That Are Futile

Revenge belongs to God.

General Patton earned the nickname he despised, "Old Blood and Guts," largely on the strength of the speeches he made to the troops, in which he portrayed action against the enemy in very graphic, very personal terms: "I cannot see any good reason for taking any prisoners—alive," he once said. And it is also true that he frequently spoke of the pleasure he would take in personally shooting Adolf Hitler ("that paper-hanging son of a bitch").

But these were things said to create hatred of the enemy. The fact is that Patton's view of war—more precisely, of victory in war, the task at hand—was thoroughly professional. Vengeance played no part in Patton's program. Winning, accomplishing the mission: that was his business. Revenge he left to God.

148. Communication Is Key

Keep a quick line of communications.

Resist the temptation to put a layer of assistants between yourself and those you are expected to lead. Establish direct, efficient two-way communication. An open-door policy is the best policy. If you cultivate an air of remoteness and unavailability, people will stop talking to you, and you will cheat yourself of the single most valuable commodity in any enterprise: information. General Patton always answered his own phone.

149. Kill Rumors with Fact

The story that spread throughout America about our tanks being inferior to German tanks finally reached the soldiers on the front lines and caused some apprehension among them. Taking two individual tanks and comparing them on a point by point basis—gun, muzzle velocity, armor protection, etc.—perhaps gives a shade to the German tank if you compared their "top" heavies to ours at that time. If the two tanks met on a village street and were to fight it out, everything else being equal, the American tank would probably have suffered. However, this was not General Patton's idea of how tanks should be used in battle. His idea was never to use tanks in a tank-to-tank fight, but to break them through the enemy lines and let them run amuck in the rear areas.

General Patton, knowing how such rumors were apt to affect adversely the morale of the troops, tried to explode the rumor before its unfortunate results took effect. The General probably knew tanks as well as any other American soldier. He had studied them intensely from their inception in World War I. He pointed out the advantage of mobility, lack of mechanical failures, power turrets, gyro stabilizers, and total numbers, in all of which we held the upper hand over the enemy. He showed where we were and with what, compared to where the enemy had retreated to and what he had left.

The results were self-evident, and General Patton's faith in the American soldier, coupled with the soldier's ingenuity, guts, and fighting ability when in an American tank, did a lot to spike the nasty rumor that was likely to affect, not only American fighting morale at the front, but also the morale of the workers at home, who were striving so hard to produce nothing but the best.

—COL. PAUL D. HARKINS ON PATTON'S HANDLING OF A POTENTIALLY DESTRUCTIVE RUMOR

There is something about members of an organization that prepares them to believe the worst about themselves and their technology. Patton knew how important it was to keep his ear to the ground for potentially destructive rumors and to scotch them when they surfaced. In this case, he used the most effective weapon for demolishing a rumor: the truth, bolstered by factual detail. He gathered and presented sufficient *relevant* factual information to allow his troops to make up their own minds. A leader can be most convincing not by *telling* people what to think, but by marshaling the appropriate facts and arguments to guide them into thinking for themselves—but in the direction desired.

150. Instructions Must Be Timely

Orders must be issued early enough to permit time to disseminate them.

In an era of e-mail and networked computers, the time-lag for dissemination of orders is probably less critical than it was during World War II; nevertheless, orders, directives, and instructions must be issued with sufficient lead time to allow their being explained (if necessary) and then carried out.

151. Instructions Should Be Personal and Direct

The best way to issue orders is by word of mouth from one general to the next. Failing this, telephone conversation which should be recorded at each end. However, in order to have a confirmatory memorandum of all oral orders given, a short written order should always be made out, not necessarily at the time of issuing the order, but it should reach the junior prior to his carrying out the order, so that, if he has forgotten anything, he will be reminded of it, and, further, in order that he may be aware that his senior has taken definite responsibility for the operation ordered orally.

It is my opinion that Army orders should not exceed a page and a half of typewritten text and it was my practice not to issue orders longer than this.

Make all of your major orders or directives in person, if possible. Especially in an age of electronic communication, person-to-person contact is extremely powerful. However, all major directives should be memorialized in writing—for the reasons Patton gives here. Finally, as Patton recommends, boil down instructions and orders. Find the fewest and best words to express what you want. This will save time, remove confusion, and minimize error.

152. Make Yourself Available and Accessible

In my opinion, generals—at least the Commanding General—should answer their own telephones in the daytime.

Many managers will find this advice radical indeed and may well resist it. But, Patton explained, answering the phone "is not particularly wearisome because few people call a general, except in emergencies, and then they like to get him at once."

Well, perhaps you get more calls than your average general. Perhaps you find it impractical to follow to the letter Patton's advice on this issue. The real point is that you should be eminently and always accessible.

153. Meetings Can Be Made to Work

Each staff should have a staff meeting, or briefing, daily, as early as the Headquarters under consideration can obtain the information for the day.

For Patton, meetings were a time to share information, and, for that reason, he believed in holding them as early as possible—provided that they were held *after* useful information had been actually obtained.

Most business organizations conduct a plethora of meetings, but too few use meetings to exchange truly useful information. Ideas are bandied about, brainstorming takes place, theories are discussed, but *information* is often a scarce commodity at meetings. Consider, then, Patton's approach: (1) The core purpose of a meeting is the exchange of information. (2) For information to be useful, it must be timely—presented in time to be acted upon.

Effective managers use meetings to coordinate the organization, not merely to trade ideas or to review the past.

154. Try a Whisper

Gen. Patton always started [a] briefing with a soft voice with several long periods of silence.

—Lt. Porter B. Williamson

Patton often peppered his speeches with "soldier talk" and profanity, but when he wanted to communicate the details of something truly important, he did what all good teachers and preachers learn to do or do naturally. He used quiet and silence. Shouting is not always the best way to get an urgent message across. Lower your voice, and people will strain to listen. They'll hang on every word. Fall silent at a critical point, and they'll wait in suspense for your next word.

155. The Power of Spontaneity

Gen. Patton never read his speech nor used any written notes, not even index cards.

—RECOLLECTIONS OF LT. PORTER B. WILLIAMSON

Develop a ready facility in public speaking, especially off the cuff. Clear, well-organized, vivid, personal communication is essential to good management. Practice. Rehearse your "spontaneity" until it really does seem spontaneous.

156. Talk the Talk

I use the language of combat soldiers. They know what I mean! Another thing, I always wear a war face. There dare not be any smiling when you give orders. War is not a smiling business. I will shoot any one of you who ever had his picture taken with a smile on his face!

—REMARKS TO HIS OFFICERS

A leader must establish identification with those he leads. He must, quite literally, speak their language. However, a leader is also an actor and must consciously *act* the part of a leader. In Patton's case, he carefully cultivated a stern mask—his "war face," which he often practiced before a mirror. Now, fortunately, most management situations do not require the studied absence of a smile; however, an effective leader must look and act the part while never becoming so wrapped up in the role that she loses touch with her "audience"—the people she manages and leads.

157. Don't Make Communication Any Harder Than It Has to Be

The decision as to whether to use clear [nonencrypted] or code radio or wire communications is very easily reached on the following basis: if the period of action is shorter than the period of reaction, use clear; otherwise use code. By this I mean that if you tell a combat team to attack at 1000 and your experience shows that the enemy cannot react to the information until 1100, use clear; and so on for higher units.

In the era before high-speed computers, messages took time to be encrypted on the sending end and decrypted on the receiving end. When sending messages in the heat of battle, the tradeoff was between secrecy and speed. Here Patton advises using common sense based on experience and the immediate situation. There is no reason to waste time encoding and decoding a message if you know that the enemy cannot make use of the information before you make use of the information. It does the enemy no good to learn of your attack *after* you have already attacked.

Managers often must make similar tradeoff decisions concerning sharing information. Make no mistake; security is important. Proprietary information must be jealously guarded. But it is also true that your colleagues and subordinates require as much information as you can give them in order to do their jobs. You must continually weigh *security* needs against the *information* needs of others in your organization. Don't base these decisions on some eternal verity in a rule book. Judge each situation individually. It does you no good to keep vital information out of the hands of your competition if, in doing so, you also fail to get that information into the hands of those who require it in your own organization.

158. Beyond Words

Every evening, Gen. Patton arranged a type of communication which united all soldiers. This "communication" united us with the soldiers of history! Gen. Patton had buglers blow Taps! Every unit down to a company of two hundred men had their own bugler. With over twenty thousand men sleeping on the ground over a thirty-mile strip of the desert valley, we had a hundred buglers.

A bugle for communication during the day in a tank outfit was as practical as a feather in a hail storm. No bugle call could be heard above the roar of the tanks and trucks, but in the stillness of the evening, a bugle call would carry for miles. With sound traveling at the rate of eleven hundred feet per second, it was impossible for all of the buglers to play Taps at the same time. It would take over five seconds for the first note of our Headquarter's bugler to reach a bugler a mile away. Thus, with a hundred buglers blowing Taps at different places and times and with the echos bouncing off the mountains, it was a sound to cause the mind of every man to pause for a moment in prayer.

Those bugle calls made us feel as if we were a part of an organization which had the power of the armies of all of the centuries.

—Lt. Porter B. Williamson, recalling life at the Desert Training Center in California

As a manager, one of your most important jobs is to provide inspiration. Each profession, each enterprise includes words, deeds, and activities that inspire top performance. Make it your business to find out just what words, deeds, and activities will inspire the people you lead. Never hesitate to make use of these things, whatever they may be.

8

“Only One Direction – Forward”

On Creating Efficiency

"The 'Old Man' hated show and sham. He was interested in one thing only — efficiency."

159. Pare Down

The successful army: First, it must fight. Second, it must eat. Third, it must be capable of rapid movement.

The effective leader always knows what he is about. Patton had an uncanny ability to distill to their core the means and ends of even the most complex of undertakings. To lead, you must understand your business at its most essential—and then be able to focus all of your resources on that essence. Here, Patton reduced the essence of an army to three elements—and he is careful to list them in order of importance.

160. Subordinate Means to Ends

The chief purpose of the General and Special Staffs is to insure that the troops get what they want in time. In battle, troops get temperamental, and ask for things which they really do not need. However, where humanly possible, their requests, no matter how unreasonable, should be answered.

General Patton demanded extraordinary things of his soldiers, driving them farther and faster than any army had ever been driven in the history of war. In exchange for this level of performance, he felt that he was getting a very good bargain by seeing to it that his troops were supplied with whatever they needed as well as with whatever extras he could get for them.

An effective leader does not bribe her subordinates, but she continually demonstrates that she cares about them and respects their wants as well as their needs. Going the extra mile to make certain that employees feel adequately rewarded—not just in terms of salary, but in the amenities that contribute to the quality of work life—will produce great dividends in the form of maximum productivity, innovation, commitment to the firm, and personal loyalty to yourself. To be sure, you cannot grant all requests, and you must not squander scarce resources. But stinginess costs far more than it saves.

161. Work Economically

Marching at night in the proximity of the enemy is not economical. It is better to halt two hours before dark, see that the men are fed, their socks dried if the weather is wet, and the vehicles serviced and made ready for the next day. Then start before dawn.

Maximum productivity is not the same as working continuously or working to exhaustion. Maximum productivity is working *economically.* It is managing time and resources efficiently. Know when to move—and know when to rest and to prepare to move. You cannot afford to squander precious human resources on creating the mere appearance of nonstop productivity.

162. Never Overlook Essential Support

Supply and administrative units and installations are frequently neglected by combat commanders. It is very necessary to their morale and efficiency that each one be inspected by the senior general of the unit with which it is operating.

Visit your back-office operations. Talk with customer-service people, fulfillment staff, and accounting departments (*your* "administrative units"), not just your sales, marketing, and R&D wizards (your "combat" units). In war, combat units get all the glory. In business, the front-office personnel occupy the spotlight. But all effective commanders realize that combat units cannot survive without the work of the administrative units, and all effective managers know that the front office is built on the foundation of the back office. Give credit where credit is due—and overdue.

163. Streamline Bureaucracy

The strength of the HQ was approximately 450 officers and 1,000 enlisted men, and Patton always ensured that these figures were never exceeded, arguing that on operations too large a staff impaired the headquarters' mobility and deprived lower units of important personnel.

—GEORGE FORTY, *THE ARMIES OF GEORGE S. PATTON*

While many World War II commanders surrounded themselves with a huge headquarters staff, Patton kept his to a minimum, always avoiding bureaucracy and never wasting resources. He believed in streamlining operations as much as possible, even if this meant sacrificing some of the trappings of high command.

164. Embrace Common Sense

Some headquarters are like merry-go-rounds. You feel as though you are going in circles, so many motions are superfluous. [In Third Army headquarters] everything was practical and for a purpose. The "Old Man" hated show and sham. He was interested in one thing only—efficiency; and his spirit permeated the whole organization. You had a feeling that Third Army was going in only one direction—forward.

—COL. BRENTON G. WALLACE, *PATTON AND HIS THIRD ARMY*

Effective leadership is efficient leadership. It pares operations down to the simplest level that is consistent with the complexity of the job at hand. That is, the methods for getting a job done should never be more complicated than necessary and certainly no more complicated than the job itself.

Take a second look at the preceding passage. Note the phrase "his spirit permeated the whole organization." While some leaders take purposeful pains to imprint their personal style on an organization and others do not, the fact is that the personality of the leader does strongly influence—*permeate*—the entire organization, whether this effect is intended or not. If you want a streamlined, efficient organization, begin by conveying these values in your own words and actions. Maybe you need to start by doing nothing more profound than clearing your desk.

165. Design for Efficiency

All Headquarters, from Regiment up to Army, should be laid out on the same general plan so that any visitor who finds himself at the Message Center will know in which direction to go to find any section.

The lesson here is to strive to create conditions of intuitive efficiency. To the extent that it is within his power, the effective manager should arrange procedures—and, yes, even work spaces—so that they are standardized in some intuitive way. Set up routine and repetitive operations so that they do not require continually reinventing the wheel. Make it possible for you and your staff to conserve physical and mental energy for the truly creative tasks.

166. Play to Your Strengths

The Americans . . . are the foremost mechanics in the world. America, as a nation, has the greatest ability for mass production of machines. It therefore behooves us to devise methods of war which exploit our inherent superiority. We must fight the war by machines on the ground, and in the air . . .

The principal management point here is straightforward: Recognize your strengths and play to them. But read a little more deeply into this statement. "It therefore behooves us to devise methods of war which will exploit our inherent superiority." Patton did not advise merely *looking* for situations in which strengths could be exploited, but also *devising* such situations. The effective leader is not content to make the most of what happens to come her way. She *devises*—invents, creates—situations tailored to her strengths and the strengths of the organization she leads. This is the essence of *proactive* management: creating circumstances rather than merely responding to them.

167. Celebrate the Back Office

All the real heroes are not storybook combat fighters either. Every single man in the Army plays a vital part. Every little job is essential to the whole scheme. What if every truck-driver suddenly decided that he didn't like the whine of those shells and turned yellow and jumped headlong into a ditch? He could say to himself, "They won't miss me—just one guy in thousands." What if every man said that? Where in the hell would we be now? No, thank God, Americans don't say that. Every man does his job. Every man serves the whole. Every department, every unit, is important to the vast scheme of things. The Ordnance is needed to supply the guns, the Quartermaster is needed to bring up the food and clothes for us—for where we are going there isn't a hell of a lot to steal! Every last damn man in the mess hall, even the one who heats the water to keep us from getting diarrhea, has a job to do. Even the Chaplain is important, for if we get killed and he is not there to bury us we would all go to hell. Each man must not only think of himself, but think of his buddy fighting alongside him. We don't want yellow cowards in the Army. They should be killed off like flies. If not, they will go back home after the war, goddam cowards, and breed more cowards. The brave men will breed more brave men. One of the bravest men I saw in the African campaign was

the fellow I saw on a telegraph pole in the midst of furious fire. . . . I stopped and asked him what the hell he was doing up there at that time. He answered, "Fixing the wire, sir." "Isn't it a little unhealthy up there right now?" I asked. "Yes, sir, but this goddam wire has got to be fixed." There was a real soldier . . . and you should have seen those trucks on the road to Gabès. The drivers were magnificent. All day they crawled along those sonofabitchin' roads, never stopping, never deviating from their course with shells bursting all around them. We got through on good old American guts. Many of the men drove over forty consecutive hours.

—SPEECH TO TROOPS PRIOR TO THE D-DAY LANDINGS AT NORMANDY

One of Patton's great gifts as a leader was the ability to prove the importance of every member of the organization. Upper management is notorious for recognizing and rewarding only front-office operations to the neglect of those who engage in support activities. Patton never made that mistake. His speeches included everyone, and he gave each member of the team a personal and individual stake in the mission. Patton understood that maintaining a team as vast as an army required walking a line between subordinating individual identity to the whole and magnifying, even glorifying the individual. An effective leader must be able to instill a similar dual vision throughout the organization: People must understand that individual action is vital, but that team work also requires subordinating ego to collective goals.

9

"Success Is How High You Can Bounce When You Hit Bottom"

On Courage and Character

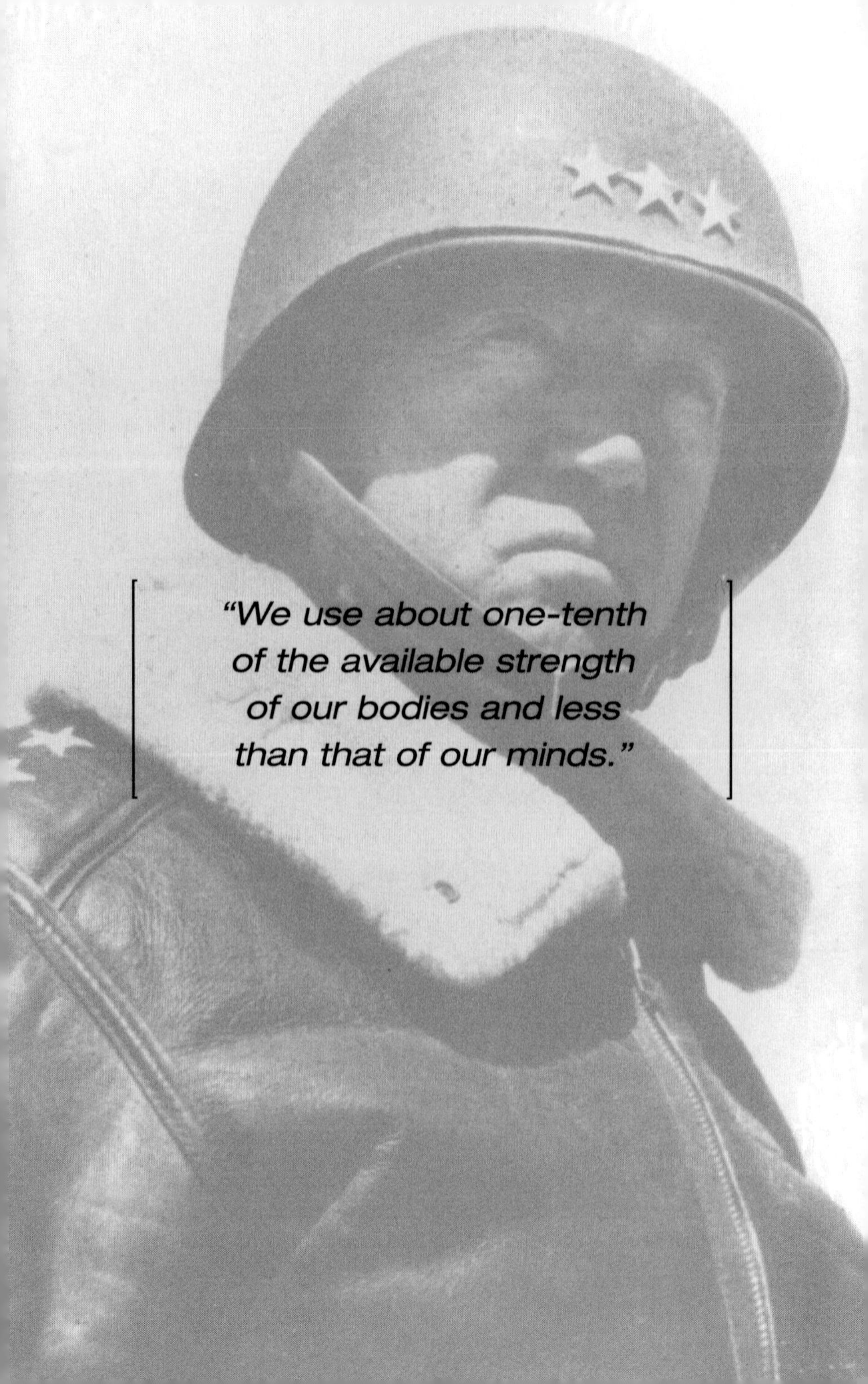
"We use about one-tenth
of the available strength
of our bodies and less
than that of our minds."

168. Make Greatness a Matter of Routine

The great things a man does appear to be great only after they are done. When they're at hand, they are normal decisions and are done without knowledge of their greatness.

This is one of Patton's most profound observations. On one level, it means that achievements can be accurately evaluated only in the fullness of time. But, more important, it also implies that a leader must make greatness second nature. That is, he or she must act in a way that recognizes that any action has potentially momentous consequences, the full import of which will not be immediately apparent. The goal? To make greatness a matter of routine.

169. Drive, Drive, Drive

You got to drive the body to the last inch of energy and then go on! You gain nothing by just going up to where your body says you are tired and exhausted. The body will build and grow only to fit the demands which the mind makes upon the lazy body. If all you do is exercise until the body is tired, the body will get lazy and stop a bit shorter every time. You have to go to the point of exhaustion and go on. That way the body will figure out, "We got to build up more body strength if that crazy mind is going to drive this hard." If you always quit when you are merely tired, you will never gain. Once you let the body tell the mind when to quit, you are whipped for sure. You cannot gain by listening to the body. We can become much stronger if we drive the body. We use about one-tenth of the available strength of our bodies and less than that of our minds!

Patton was an Olympic competitor in 1912 and a lifelong athlete. He believed that a leader could not afford to be out of shape and that a flabby body created a flabby mind. But, even more, he believed in stretching oneself, in always pushing the envelope. He would have agreed with the poet Robert Browning that "a man's reach should exceed his grasp."

Only by stretching do we grow. If you push the limits, you define new limits. And then you should push *those*. We are capable of producing and achieving much more than we believe possible.

170. Cultivate Independence

Lack of orders is no excuse for inaction.

By definition, a leader takes the initiative and acts whenever necessary. He or she does not wait to be told what to do. The exceptional leader cultivates this proactive approach in others by establishing flexible guidelines that can serve in the absence of direct, detailed instructions. Patton always made such "standing orders" crystal clear.

171. Focus on Purpose

If you want to be a Napoleon, always think of the mission first! Forget about Army Regulations. Army Regulations are written by those who have never been in battle. They write about what they have been told by others.

The lesson to learn here is *not* to violate your organization's rules and procedures, but to beware of following abstract theory and received wisdom slavishly. Real situations require flexibility and spontaneity. Rules, rules of thumb, and sage advice from on high are all well and good—use them as guides—but be prepared to act spontaneously in the interests of the immediate "mission." This takes courage and sound judgment. It separates the leaders who are truly leaders from the "managers" who merely follow the "rules" others have laid down.

172. Do What Must Be Done

At 1330 on the afternoon of November 11, 1942, Admiral Michelier, the Supreme French Commander in West Africa, and General Nogués, the Resident General, came with their staffs to the Hotel Miramar at Fedhala to surrender. When I left Washington, I had been provided with two sets of surrender conditions, one more lenient than the other. I had, naturally, read them several times on the trip across, but owing to a lack of historical knowledge, did not realize until the French arrived that the conditions were drawn for Algiers, which is a French Department, whereas Morocco is a protectorate where the prestige of the French Army is the only thing holding the Arabs in check. In view of this fact it was evident to me that neither set of conditions was applicable.

The situation was further complicated by the fact that I was out of all communication with General Eisenhower and had no knowledge as to how the other attacks in Africa were progressing. I had to make a decision, and I had to maintain Morocco as a gateway for the Americans entering the continent of Africa. Morocco could not be used as a gateway if it were in the throes of an Arab uprising. Hence I had to maintain the prestige of the French Army.

I got up and said, in my not too good French, that I was a former student at the French Cavalry School, that I had served with the French for two years in World War I, and that I had great respect for and belief in the word of honor of a French officer, and that if the French officers present would give me their word of honor that they would not fire against American troops or American ships, they could retain their weapons, man their seacoast forts, and carry on in all respects as they had carried on previously—but under my orders.

I have never had reason to regret my decision. Had I done otherwise, I am convinced that at least sixty thousand American troops would have had to occupy Morocco; thereby preventing our using it to the maximum and reducing our already inadequate forces.

Leadership is put to the test in situations such as the one Patton describes here. When your instructions do not match the situation at hand, you must either exercise initiative or suffer paralysis. The key phrase in the passage quoted is "I had to make a decision." That is what a leader *has* to do. Furthermore, even in the absence of instructions from higher authority, Patton understood the nature of the decision he *had* to make: "I had to maintain Morocco as a gateway for the Americans entering the continent of Africa." With this understanding, Patton found the moral and mental strength to make the necessary decision.

When higher authority is clear and available, it is the manager's job to act in accordance with higher authority. But in situations where such authority is unavailable, it is the manager's job to take command of a situation so thoroughly that he or she can make the best independent decision. The alternative is paralysis. Even so, the price of such decisions can be high and may even come at a personal cost. In the case of Patton's action in Morocco, the decision was all to the good. At the end of the war in Europe, however, Patton made a similar decision when he was serving as military governor of the occupied German province of Bavaria. Despite a standing Allied order to "de-Nazify" all civil government, Patton decided that the former Nazi officials were the only people who possessed the experience and training to maintain orderly operation of the basic services the German citizens needed to survive after the defeat of their nation. He therefore refused to follow through with de-Nazification. As a result, he was vilified in the popular press and ultimately removed from command of his beloved Third Army.

173. Accept Accountability for Your Decisions

He never used his stars to cover his errors.

—M.Sgt. John L. Mims, Patton's personal driver from September 1940 to May 1945

You know the old saying: To err is human, to forgive, divine. When you make a mistake, give the people you work with—including those you supervise—a shot at divinity. Admit your error. Own up. Then propose a course to correct the mistake. Never use your authority to mask mistakes. Admit them. Explain them. Apologize for them. Above all else, *use* them. Allow people to see how you accept responsibility and how you can learn from error. However, do not overanalyze mistakes or indulge in endless rounds of *woulda, shoulda, coulda.* Once you admit an error, look to the future. What have you learned? How will you keep this from happening again?

174. Demand Accountability from Others

"When you make a mistake in war, the punishment is death! The trouble is your mistake could cause hundreds of soldiers to die. In war, the enemy does not give a warning before they shoot! That's not the way war works. If the enemy sees you first, he shoots first!"

In our staff meetings Gen. Patton advised instant punishment for every mistake. Often a staff member would go to the defense of a friend and suggest some softer punishment. When some officer with a degree in management would explain the new ideas for leadership, Gen. Patton would explode, "All that 'save the ego' nonsense is not for leadership in war. A dead man does not have any ego! How long after you touch a burning match does it take before you get burned? You get your punishment instantly by touching the match. That is the way Mother Nature works, and that's the way war works. What happens to the tree that does not put down its roots? Such a tree will die for lack of water or blow over with the first strong wind. Every mistake has its own punishment. How long does it take for a garden rake to hit you in the face when you step on the teeth turned

toward you? Didn't you ever stub your toe on a rock? How long after your toe hits the rock does it take for you to feel the pain?"

—Lt. Porter B. Williamson

Punishment is not something most management texts talk about, and in most management contexts, punishment is not a viable option for shaping behavior. However, analysis and correction of errors and inappropriate actions is an important part of management, and the point to be learned here is that such analysis and correction must come quickly and must be made without flinching. Business can be highly unforgiving. Unlike in war, an error will probably not result in death, but it may result in substantial losses of money, time, opportunity, and other resources. As the "natural" consequences of error are unforgiving and often instantaneous, so your response to error and poor judgment should be frank and immediate.

175. Courage Is No Stranger to Fear

If we take the generally accepted definition of bravery as a quality which knows not fear, I have never seen a brave man.

General Patton never hesitated to tell his troops that he was afraid. "All men are frightened," he pointed out. "The more intelligent they are, the more they are frightened. The courageous man is the man who forces himself, in spite of his fear, to carry on. Discipline, pride, self-respect, self-confidence, and the love of glory are attributes which will make a man courageous even when he is afraid."

If you think that business is not about life and death, you are deceiving yourself. True, bullets aren't whizzing by, and shells aren't exploding, but your career and success hang on every decision you make. Don't deny your fears. Don't try to run away from them. Carry on in spite of them.

176. Act Beyond Your Fears

Do not take counsel of your fears.

Patton never denied being fearful in battle. Quite the contrary: he admitted to fear. He admitted to fear, and he advised others to admit to fear and to recognize their fear—but, having recognized it, never to "take counsel" of it. Patton believed that a good commander is one who learns to live with fear, to control it so that fear is never put in the driver's seat. You cannot learn to avoid fear, but you can learn to recognize when you are in danger of acting in blind accordance with it. You can learn not to take counsel of fear. Thus, in any effective leader, "courage" is more a learned skill than it is an inborn trait.

177. Daring Fuels Enterprise

Daring is wisdom. It is the highest part of war.

—FROM PATTON'S WEST POINT NOTEBOOK

Creative risk taking is essential to success in any enterprise with stakes worth the winning. Thoughtless risks are destructive, of course, but perhaps even more wasteful is thoughtless caution, which prompts inaction and promotes failure to seize opportunity.

178. Make Courage a Habit

Courage is largely habit and self-confidence.

Courage is a valuable commodity on the battlefield or in the board room. Patton believed that it could be learned—acquired through practice. He worked at making courage a habit, the rule governing his behavior, rather than the exception.

179. Moral Courage

Moral courage is the most valuable and usually the most absent characteristic in men.

Like most soldiers, Patton distinguished two types of courage: the physical courage that enables a person to face bullets in battle and the moral courage that enables a person to stand up for what he or she believes in and for what he or she knows is right. Contrary to what too many believe, good business is not incompatible with good morals. Establish a high standard for fairness and decency and you will create a work environment of trust and support, which will empower everyone to take the intelligent risks necessary to advance any enterprise. No one sticks his neck out if he senses that it may be chopped from behind.

180. Bounce

In our great country, most any fool can be a success at something. Look at the flag pole climbers and gold fish eaters! The problem with success is that it leads to failure. When you are on top, there is no place to go but down. . . . Success is how high you can bounce when you hit bottom.

For some, success is a powerful fuel that drives greater and greater success. For others, it is a narcotic that dulls further action. No leader who rests on his or her laurels remains a leader.

As if you even *could* rest on them!

Everyone fails. But that doesn't mean you must identify yourself as a failure. Failure applies to a situation, a particular time and place. If you don't let it devastate you, failure can be an opportunity—for learning, for recovery, for the creation and demonstration of character. No general expects to win every battle. Each learns to take his losses, learn from them if possible, and move on. The same is true in any enterprise involving risk. You cannot avoid failure all of the time, but you can refuse to be pinned down by it.

As Patton observed, when you are on top, there is no place to go but down. True success is character, and character is measured by how high you bounce when you topple from that height and hit bottom.

10

"Audacity"

On Managing the Impossible

“The impossible place is usually the least well defended.”

181. The Miracle of Audacity

In war nothing is impossible, provided you use audacity.

Patton was fond of quoting the eighteenth-century Prussian emperor and military genius Frederick the Great, who advised commanders thus: *"L'audace, l'audace, toujours l'audace."* Audacity, audacity, always audacity.

In modern usage, the word *audacity* is more often than not negative, signifying insolence, carelessness, or heedlessness. But Patton used it in an earlier sense, in the way that Frederick would have appreciated: fearlessness, daring, intrepidity—heedless, indeed, but specifically heedless of conventional restraints.

Few business people are comfortable with the idea of audacity, yet without it, little of great merit can be accomplished. The stakes of audacity are doubtless high, because the price of failure is great. Yet the price of avoiding audacity is high as well: a long, drawn-out consignment to mediocrity.

182. The Impossible Place Is Usually the Least Well Defended

On the twenty-fifth [of March 1945], the 87th Division succeeded in making its crossing and had two regiments over the river by daylight, in spite of the fact that all the historical studies we had ever read on the crossing asserted that, between Bingen and Coblentz, the Rhine was impassable. Here again we took advantage of a theory of our own, that the impossible place is usually the least well defended.

Patton valued the lessons of the past and was an intense and avid student of history, yet he departed sharply from precedent when he believed he had a better idea. A true leader, he was a bold innovator and used innovation to surprise the enemy.

You cannot take your competition by surprise if you act exclusively on precedent and received wisdom. Look at the situation afresh and always consider the advantages of taking the road less traveled.

183. Do Something About the Weather

The weather was so bad that I directed all Army chaplains to pray for dry weather. I also published a prayer with a Christmas greeting on the back and sent it to all members of the Command. The prayer was for dry weather for battle.

Patton left no stone unturned in the effort to create conditions favorable to his army's enterprises. On the eve of the desperate Battle of the Bulge, on or about December 14, 1944, he called the Third Army chaplain into his office:

> GENERAL PATTON: *"Chaplain, I want you to publish a prayer for good weather. I'm tired of these soldiers having to fight mud and floods as well as Germans. See if we can't get God to work on our side."*
>
> CHAPLAIN O'NEILL: *"Sir, It's going to take a pretty thick rug for that kind of praying."*
>
> GENERAL PATTON: *"I don't care if it takes a flying carpet. I want the praying done."*
>
> CHAPLAIN O'NEILL: *"Yes, sir. May I say, General, that it usually isn't a customary thing among men of my profession to pray for clear weather to kill fellow men."*

General Patton: "Chaplain, are you teaching me theology or are you the Chaplain of the Third Army? I want a prayer."

Chaplain O'Neill: "Yes, sir."

Outside, the chaplain said, "Whew, that's a tough one! What do you think he wants?"

It was perfectly clear to me [recalled Col. Paul D. Harkins, Patton's chief of staff]. The General wanted a prayer—he wanted one right now—and he wanted it published to the Command.

The Army Engineer was called in, and we finally decided that our field topographical company could print the prayer on a small-sized card, making enough copies for distribution to the army.

It being near Christmas, we also decided to ask General Patton to include a Christmas greeting to the troops on the same card with the prayer. The General agreed, wrote a short greeting, and the card was made up, published, and distributed to the troops on the twenty-second of December.

Actually, the prayer was offered in order to bring clear weather for the planned Third Army break-through to the Rhine in the Saarguemines area, then scheduled for December 21.

The Bulge put a crimp in these plans. As it happened, the Third Army had moved north to attack the south flank of the Bulge when the prayer was actually issued.

PRAYER

Almighty and most merciful Father, we humbly beseech Thee, of Thy great goodness, to restrain these immoderate rains with which we have had to contend. Grant us fair weather for battle. Graciously hearken to us as soldiers who call upon Thee that, armed with Thy power, we may advance from victory to victory, and crush the oppression and wickedness of our enemies, and establish Thy justice among men and nations. Amen.

REVERSE SIDE

To each officer and soldier in the Third United States Army, I wish a Merry Christmas. I have full confidence in your courage, devotion to duty, and skill in battle. We march in our might to complete victory. May God's blessing rest upon each of you on this Christmas Day.

G. S. Patton, Jr.
Lieutenant General
Commanding, Third United States Army

A highly effective way to affirm your leadership is to preside over celebration and commemoration. Create special events from time to time, and always greet your subordinates and colleagues on major holidays.

Patton's combination prayer and Christmas card created a sensation with his troops. As to the rains, they stopped the day after the prayer was issued; Patton pinned a Bronze Star on the chaplain: "Chaplain, you're the most popular man in this Headquarters. You sure stand in good with the Lord and soldiers."

Recommended Reading

The following books are indispensible to anyone seriously interested in Patton. These are the sources of most of the quotations reproduced in Patton on Leadership.

Allen, Robert S. *Drive to Victory.* New York: Berkley, 1947.

Anders, Curt. *Fighting Generals.* New York: Putnam, 1965.

Army Times Editors. *Warrior: The Story of General George S. Patton.* New York: Putnam, 1967.

Blumenson, Martin. *Kasserine Pass.* Boston: Houghton Mifflin, 1967.

___. *Patton: The Man Behind the Legend, 1885–1945.* New York: Morrow, 1985.

___. *The Patton Papers, 1885–1940.* Boston: Houghton Mifflin, 1972.

___. *The Patton Papers, 1940–1945.* Boston: Houghton Mifflin, 1974.

Bradley, Omar N. *A Soldier's Story.* New York: Henry Holt, 1951.

Carpenter, Allan. *George Smith Patton, Jr.* Vero Beach, FL: Rourke Publications, 1987.

Codman, Charles R. *Drive.* Boston: Little, Brown and Co., Inc., 1957.

D'Este, Carlo. *Patton: A Genius for War.* New York: HarperCollins, 1995.

Dyer, George. *XII Corps: Spearhead of Patton's Third Army.* Baton Rouge, LA: Army Navy Publishing Co., 1947.

Essame, H. *Patton: The Commander.* London: B. T. Batsford, 1974.

Forty, George. *The Armies of George S. Patton.* London: Arms and Armour Press, 1996.

___. *Patton's Third Army at War.* New York: Scribners, 1978.

Harkins, Paul D. *When the Third Cracked Europe.* Harrisburg, PA: Stackpole, 1969.

Hatch, Alden. *George Patton: General in Spurs.* New York: Julian Messner, 1950.

Mellor, William Bancroft. *General Patton: The Last Cavalier.* New York: Putnam, 1971.

___. *Patton, Fighting Man.* New York: Putnam, 1946.

Odom, Charles B. *General George S. Patton and Eisenhower.* New Orleans: Word Picture Productions, 1985.

Patton, George S., Jr. *War as I Knew It.* 1947; reprint ed., New York: Bantam, 1980.

Pearl, Jack. *Blood and Guts Patton.* New York: Monarch, 1961.

Province, Charles M. *Patton's One-Minute Messages: Tactical Leadership Skills for Business Managers.* Novato, CA: Presidio Press, 1995.

___. *The Unknown Patton.* New York: Bonanza, 1983.

Semmes, Harry H. *Portrait of Patton.* New York: Appleton-Century-Crofts, 1955.

Truscott, Lucian K. *Command Missions.* New York: E. P. Dutton, 1954.

Wedemeyer, Albert C. *Wedemeyer Reports!* New York: Henry Holt, 1958.

Whiting, Charles. *Patton.* New York: Ballantine, 1970.

Williamson, Porter B. *General Patton's Principles for Life and Leadership.* Tucson, AZ: MSC, 1988.

Index

D

E

I

J

K

L

M

N

O

Q

R

S

T

U

V

W

Acknowledgments

Special thanks to the Patton Museum of Cavalry and Armor, Fort Knox, Kentucky, and to the museum's librarian, Candace L. Fuller, for furnishing photographs of General Patton in action.

Thanks to Barry Richardson of Prentice Hall for special contributions to this book.

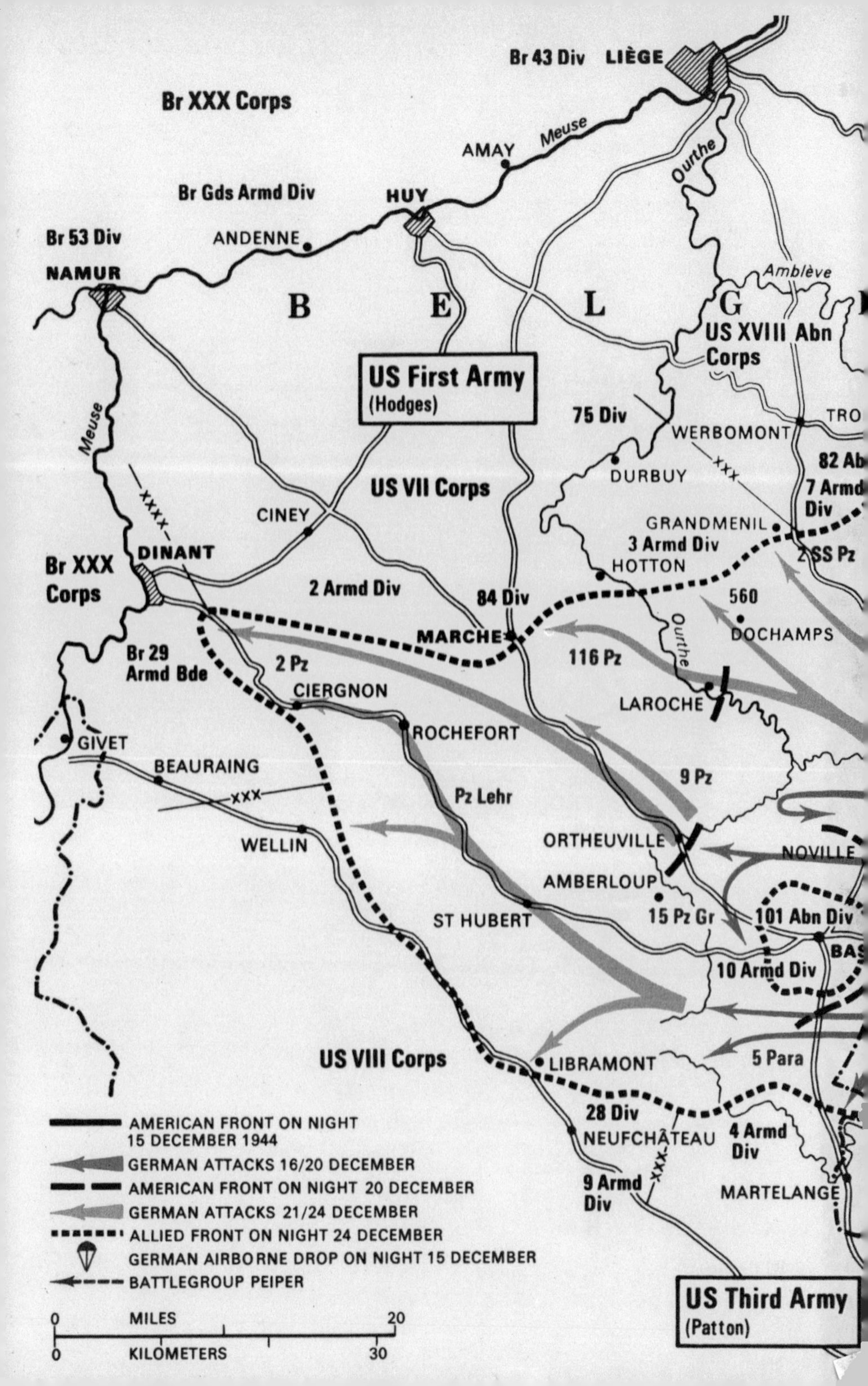

Br 43 Div
LIÈGE
Br XXX Corps
Meuse
AMAY
Ourthe
Br Gds Armd Div
HUY
Br 53 Div
ANDENNE
NAMUR
Amblève
B E L G
US XVIII Abn Corps
US First Army (Hodges)
75 Div
WERBOMONT
TRO
Meuse
DURBUY
82 Ab
7 Armd Div
US VII Corps
CINEY
GRANDMENIL
3 Armd Div
2 SS Pz
DINANT
HOTTON
Br XXX Corps
2 Armd Div
84 Div
560
MARCHE
DOCHAMPS
Br 29 Armd Bde
2 Pz
116 Pz
Ourthe
CIERGNON
LAROCHE
GIVET
ROCHEFORT
BEAURAING
9 Pz
Pz Lehr
WELLIN
ORTHEUVILLE
NOVILLE
AMBERLOUP
15 Pz Gr
101 Abn Div
ST HUBERT
BAS
10 Armd Div
US VIII Corps
LIBRAMONT
5 Para
28 Div
NEUFCHÂTEAU
4 Armd Div
9 Armd Div
MARTELANGE
AMERICAN FRONT ON NIGHT 15 DECEMBER 1944
GERMAN ATTACKS 16/20 DECEMBER
AMERICAN FRONT ON NIGHT 20 DECEMBER
GERMAN ATTACKS 21/24 DECEMBER
ALLIED FRONT ON NIGHT 24 DECEMBER
GERMAN AIRBORNE DROP ON NIGHT 15 DECEMBER
BATTLEGROUP PEIPER
0 MILES 20
0 KILOMETERS 30
US Third Army (Patton)